HOOSIER
BEGINNINGS

HOOSIER BEGINNINGS

*The Birth of
Indiana University
Athletics*

KEN BIKOFF

WELL HOUSE
BOOKS

INDIANA UNIVERSITY PRESS

This book is a publication of

Indiana University Press
Office of Scholarly Publishing
Herman B Wells Library 350
1320 East 10th Street
Bloomington, Indiana 47405 USA

iupress.org

© 2020 by Indiana University Press
All rights reserved

No part of this book may be reproduced or utilized in any form or by any means, electronic or mechanical, including photocopying and recording, or by any information storage and retrieval system, without permission in writing from the publisher. The paper used in this publication meets the minimum requirements of the American National Standard for Information Sciences—Permanence of Paper for Printed Library Materials, ANSI Z39.48–1992.

Manufactured in the United States of America

Cataloging information is available from the Library of Congress.

ISBN 978-0-253-05047-2 (cloth)
ISBN 978-0-253-05048-9 (paper)
ISBN 978-0-253-05049-6 (ebook)

First printing 2020

To Nick and Charlie—

NOTHING NEW EVER HAPPENS,
BUT YOU CAN BE UNIQUE.
GO MAKE HISTORY.

Contents

Preface	ix
1. In the Beginning . . . Athletics Arrive in Bloomington	1
2. The Arrival of Football and a New Home	24
3. The Birth of IU Basketball	50
4. Tragedy and Triumph	73
5. The Baseball Riot	97
6. Money Problems and a Massive Improvement	105
7. A God in Bloomington	131
8. Jumbo . . . and What Might Have Been	148
9. What's in a Name?	168
10. The Old Stolen Bucket	177
Sources	187
Index	191

Preface

I'm surrounded by ghosts. I always have been.

I haven't always seen them, but they've always been there. They aren't rattling chains or knocking on floors at all hours of the night. I don't need to call Bill Murray and his friends to come bust anything. But everywhere I look, there are ghosts.

They're around you, too.

That's what history is to me. Real ghosts. I can walk down Tenth Street on the campus of Indiana University toward the Herman B Wells Library, and I don't just see Woodlawn Field and some intramural soccer goals. I don't just see the Arboretum. I don't just see what used to be known as the HPER when I was a student in Bloomington from 1993 to 1997.

Instead, I see the golf course that used to be in the area of the Arboretum and Woodlawn Field back when all of it was called Dunn Meadow. Dunn Meadow still exists, of course, as a far smaller area in front of the Indiana Memorial Union, and they used to play tennis there . . . but I digress.

The ghosts get in the way all the time.

Back on Tenth Street, I see the original Memorial Stadium where the Arboretum stands. I can look at the HPER building and imagine an apple orchard blocking my view of the landscape, and I can nearly hear the sound of axes chopping down trees to reshape the campus.

I can walk past Ernie Pyle Hall, where I spent so many hours as an undergrad pursuing my degree from the then School of Journalism, and I don't just see a parking lot outside of the Union. I see Jordan Field and imagine

Jim Thorpe and Jimmy Sheldon and Cotton Berndt setting the foundation for football at the university.

I can walk behind the union and see the carpenter's shop that was the original gymnasium, where the first practices for IU basketball were held. I can walk through a parking lot where the original Assembly Hall stood, and I can read a marker that tells the story of what used to be there—a marker I had a part in getting placed on campus.

The ghosts are there. You just have to know to look for them.

I'm consistently frustrated by history, too.

I wish so desperately that I could have watched a game at Jordan Field, that I could have cheered on IU at the original Assembly Hall, that I could have seen the buildings on the Seminary Square campus. They are all still real to me, and although they no longer exist, I feel a compulsion to keep them alive.

People love history. They really do. They just don't tend to like it the way it was taught to them in school.

Dates aren't history, no matter what your lazy history teacher told you when you were in class just trying to stay awake. In the who-what-when-where-why-how equation, the when might be the least important part. It's a fact—nothing more, nothing less.

Memorizing facts isn't history. It's trivia. History is a story. It's right there in the word.

History explains the world. It explains the chain of events that leads people to lay out their hard-earned money for tickets, put on candy-striped pants, drive to a midwestern university, and walk into a building built solely for the purpose of hosting people to watch a silly children's game in which someone throws a ball through a ring of iron.

History informs us where we've been and provides a guide for what may come. History predicts the future if you read it right, if you care enough to make the effort.

Ultimately, nothing new ever happens. Ever.

The biggest reason I consistently find myself frustrated by history is that so many people seem to think the world began the day they were born. Millions of students have walked by the Arboretum, never realizing Memorial Stadium once stood there. It doesn't cross their mind to wonder what the campus looked like ten or fifty or one hundred years earlier. They don't think twice about those who have taken those same steps before them, whether it was a day earlier, a month earlier, a year earlier, or a century earlier.

Yet each one of those ghosts led those students to the IU campus, sometimes literally. A chance meeting on band day at an IU football game may have led to a student's grandparents meeting, and their shared love of IU and each other set into motion a chain of events that led to a student walking down Tenth Street on his or her way to class.

The seed of this book was planted in the late 2000s when I was working as editor-in-chief of *Inside Indiana Magazine*. I was strolling through a bookstore and flipped through a copy of the *Bloomington and Indiana University* edition of the Images of America series of books. It's essentially a history of an area told mostly through pictures.

There on one of the pages was a photo of the Faris family farm. The caption read, "The Faris house and farm occupied the site until 1956, when these photographs were taken and the site was purchased by Indiana University. ... The Seventeenth Street Football Stadium was completed here in 1960. In 1971, it was renamed Memorial Stadium. Assembly Hall is located nearby on the east side of the site."

Later that same day, I called my boss, the late, great publisher of *Inside Indiana*, Ed Magoni, and told him I wanted to do a story about the history of the athletic facilities at IU. He thought it sounded like a good idea.

"It will be just one story," I said.

I was wrong.

Over the next year, I put together a thirteen-part series on the history of every major athletic facility on IU's campus. The games that were played were a footnote. I was focused on how the facilities came to be.

That blossomed into a number of other history stories, leading me down a rabbit hole I hope I never escape. You'll read some of the stories in this book.

In May 2017, I was invited to speak to the Bloomington Rotary Club to tell some of my stories. I called the presentation "A Short, Unorganized History of IU Athletics."

Following my first presentation, I was approached by someone asking if I had ever thought about putting together a book of the stories. It had crossed my mind, but I didn't have the slightest idea about how to go about getting a book published.

The next day, I received an email from a representative at IU Press, saying she had been tipped off about a possible book idea, and IU Press would like to talk to me about it.

That's the history of this book.

My vision for this book is very much like the original presentation. It's a short, unorganized history of early IU athletics, basically from 1867 to 1930. I didn't set out to provide a season-by-season rundown of results and dates in the various sports. I didn't try to cover everything.

I'm not in it for the trivia. I'm in it for the stories.

My goal is to answer questions that you didn't know you had. Ever wonder why the school is called Indiana University and not the University of Indiana? Have you thought about how IU basketball came about? Any idea why IU's colors are cream and crimson or why IU's teams are nicknamed the Hoosiers?

Maybe you have wondered. Maybe you haven't. But my hope is that I can answer some of those questions in an entertaining way that also allows you to brag to your friends that you know something they don't know.

Because really, that's what history is. It is stories told by one person to another, who then passes it on to another and another and another. History comes alive through stories, and I certainly aim to resurrect some of the long-buried history of IU athletics.

Before we get to those stories, I wanted to thank a few people for their help in making this book a reality.

My wife, Lauren, far and away deserves more credit than anyone else. That poor woman has had to deal with my IU obsession since the day she met me. She moved two hundred miles away from her family to join me in Bloomington when I had the opportunity to cover IU sports, and she has endured countless nights home alone as I was covering games. She has had to listen to me talk about the things I've pulled from the dustbin of time or yanked out of a book over and over again, and she has listened with a nod and a smile despite the fact she honestly couldn't care less about any of it.

I want to thank Mike Pegram of Peegs.com and Ed Magoni of *Inside Indiana* for making my time in Bloomington possible. Peegs connected me to Ed, who started me down this path, and Ed's enthusiasm for my story ideas—and his willingness to go along with my passion—made this book happen. Ed is no longer with us, but this book is as much a testament to him as it is to any work I've done.

Jim Shea, the former senior director of planning and communications at the Luddy School of Informatics, Computing, and Engineering, deserves credit, too. It was Jim who invited me to speak at the Rotary Club meeting, and without his invitation, this book would have never happened. Jim Bright, a former president of the Bloomington Press Club and the man who suggested I put my stories into a book, deserves just as much credit. It was his push that moved this book from a vague idea down the path to reality.

I also want to thank Indiana University Press for making this book happen, as well as Ashley Runyon, Peggy Solic, Michelle Mastro, and Gary Dunham for their help with everything. Brad Cook, the curator of photographs at the IU Archives, has been a tremendous help over the years in providing the visuals to go along with my words; and Dina Kellams, the director of university archives, has helped me in so many ways with this project and many more. Brad and Dina do it with a smile and a graciousness that is rare in this world.

Let's go find some ghosts.

HOOSIER
BEGINNINGS

1

In the Beginning...Athletics Arrive in Bloomington

Let's start at the beginning, which is a very good place to start.

Simply put, Indiana University is unique. Sure, every university believes itself to be special, and alumni everywhere believe their college or university is somehow set apart from the rest.

When it comes to IU, it just happens to be true.

It starts with the name.

Have you ever wondered why it's "Indiana University" and not the "University of Indiana"? After all, IU is one of just a handful of schools that don't follow the "University of . . ." template that is the hallmark of state flagship schools. In fact, Indiana University is one of just seven state flagship schools—the others being Louisiana State, Rutgers, SUNY Buffalo, The Ohio State University, Penn State, and West Virginia—that don't follow the "University of . . ." pattern.

But what makes IU unique, truly one of a kind, is that Indiana University is the only non-land-grant state flagship university in the nation that doesn't follow the "University of . . ." template. Rutgers University—which actually is officially named Rutgers, The State University of New Jersey—comes closest to matching IU. It was established as Queen's College in 1766, went through a few name changes, and was named the sole land-grant college in 1864. Rutgers didn't become a university until 1924.

But Indiana University has been known by that name since 1838, and the story of why, exactly, IU is Indiana University instead of the University of Indiana is a study in convenience.

Again, to get to the answer, we have to start at the beginning.

Indiana was admitted to the union December 11, 1816, as the nineteenth of the United States of America. The state constitution, adopted the previous summer, required the establishment of a state school or seminary, but the land for the institution couldn't be provided until the start of 1820. As soon as January 1820 rolled around, the young state legislature proposed an "act to establish a State Seminary, and for other purposes," which was passed January 20, 1820.

That date has been celebrated at IU first as Foundation Day and later as Founders Day, with annual events commemorating the establishment of the school.

Not that anything really happened that day outside of some legislative paperwork. In fact, it would take years for the State Seminary to get up and running.

The establishment of a school takes time. Land has to be procured, buildings have to be planned, and construction has to take place. And although the bureaucratic red tape didn't exist at quite the same level as it does now, it still took some time to get the State Seminary up and running.

Five years, in fact.

The campus's first buildings—the Seminary Building and the Professor's House—began construction in 1822 in Bloomington, Indiana, and an advertisement for the State Seminary appeared in a Madison, Indiana, newspaper that same year. The Professor's House was completed in 1824, offering a place for the State Seminary's only professor, Baynard Rush Hall, to live.

On April 4, 1825, ten students began classes in ancient Greek and Latin in the Seminary Building on what became known as Seminary Square, currently in the area of the intersection of Second and College Avenues in Bloomington. Seminary Square is a public park, and the area that held the first campus of IU now features a grocery store and other businesses.

Indiana University had been born.

But it wouldn't stay a State Seminary for long. Hoping to expand what it could offer to students, and with an eye on providing more opportunities for the citizens of Indiana, changes would have to be made. On January 24, 1828, the Indiana state legislature reorganized the State Seminary into the Indiana College, promoting the education of youth in the "American, learned and foreign languages, the useful arts, sciences, and literature."

Andrew Wylie was elected president by the newly formed board of trustees on May 4, 1828; accepted the position in May 1829; and was inaugurated as the first president of Indiana College on October 29, 1829. In 1830, construction began on the first Indiana College building, which housed the chapel, the library, and some classrooms. Wylie's House—which still stands to this day—was finished in 1835.

The college continued to expand, and the first dormitory was built in 1838. It was attached to the Professor's House.

So much for independent living.

But that same year—on February 15, 1838, to be exact—the Indiana General Assembly passed an act changing the name of the school for what would be the final time. The Indiana College, which began as the State Seminary of Indiana just eighteen years earlier, would henceforth be known as Indiana University.

Why was the name changed? Well, it seems purely aesthetic. In his book *Indiana University: Midwestern Pioneer, Volume 1: The Early Years*, Thomas D. Clark, former historian at IU, said that "one searches the record in vain for some expression of an enlarged educational philosophy, significant curriculum change, or faculty expansion" following the change.

Bottom line: the name just sounded better and more prestigious. So the change was made, and the way it was made set Indiana University apart. It seems like a natural progression—State Seminary to State College to State University—but the name itself is so rare that it is routinely misstated as the University of Indiana by everyone from major news outlets to NFL teams to the general public.

Regardless of the confusion, IU, by its very name, is a unique institution.

The rise of organized athletics at IU mirrored that of American society at large. Life on the frontier wasn't exactly filled with opportunities for leisure. Free time wasn't in abundance, especially in the developing state of Indiana. From the school's birth in 1820 until the Civil War, athletics at IU were nonexistent. There may have been some leisure activities on campus, but they weren't organized in any serious way.

That changed in 1866.

When the fall semester of 1866 rolled around, Indiana University was a quiet place. There were just 112 students enrolled for classes, every one of them a man (women were allowed to take in some lectures, but the first woman student wouldn't enroll until the next year). Among those 112 men was Malcolm Andrew "Mack" McDonald, who grew up in Williamsport, Indiana, and was the son of Joseph E. McDonald. Two years earlier, Joseph had run unsuccessfully as the Democratic candidate for governor of the state of Indiana, and he would later become a one-term US Senator.

McDonald grew up on North Pennsylvania Street in Indianapolis, opposite University Square, and was friends with Aquilla Jones, who lived in the neighborhood and had learned to play baseball during his time at a prep school in Farmington, Maine.

In the April 7, 1917, edition of the *"I" Men's Notes*—a regular publication from the "I" Men, an organization of former athletes who had lettered in a sport at IU—McDonald claimed to have organized the first baseball game in the state of Indiana "between the Western baseball club of Indianapolis and the Wabash baseball club of Lafayette at Lafayette in 1863." McDonald said he played third base in the game.

When McDonald and Jones enrolled at IU, they took their love of the game with them.

"When I arrived at the University in 1866, everything pertaining to baseball was very crude indeed in the whole country as compared with today," McDonald said.

> The ball was much larger, heavier, and very "lively." There were no regulation bats, no gloves, no masks, and no pads or shields of any kind used. The home plate was almost any kind of a piece of flat iron of most any size, and the bases were bags stuffed with hay or straw. No batter's position was defined; you could stand at bat most any way the umpire said. The pitcher's position was two parallel lines four feet apart, first line 27-feet, 9-inches from the home plate. Each player furnished his own bat that he turned out of any kind of wood which suited him and almost any length of size he fancied. The first diamond was laid off southeast of the college, the catcher facing the college about 500 feet from the building.

The games weren't really organized yet, and baseball was still in the process of catching on. Those who enjoyed playing gathered most afternoons throughout the fall of 1866. By the next spring, McDonald helped organize the first athletic team in IU history, and Jones was part of the squad.

McDonald wrote: "The regular team was (Edwin) McIntire, catcher; Allison Maxwell, 1st base; Richard Maxwell, 2nd base; Fred Howe, 3rd base; McDonald and Jones, pitchers; (John) Rice, shortstop; Frank Hall, William Bynum, Homer Bothwell, Arthur Twineham, and Shannon Nave, fielders. We had a number of other members of the club, but these I have mentioned were the most prominent players and showed more talent in the game."

Other players included Joseph Wright, James Jordan, Henry Gilmore, Harley Sutton, Warren Sherman, and Harry Kertz. McDonald was the captain of the team, and he earned the nickname "the father of baseball at Indiana." That role, however, would be questioned by none other than IU president William Lowe Bryan, but more on that below.

Baseball at IU was a young man's game. Hall was the only senior on the team, and Maxwell was the only junior. The rest of the players mentioned by McDonald were freshmen and sophomores, and three of the players—Rice, Nave, and Jones—were part of the Preparatory Department, which worked as a form of a modern high school to fill in gaps of knowledge for students before they entered regular college classes.

On April 20, 1867, the students issued a request to the faculty to use the southwest corner of the Seminary Square campus as a baseball diamond. The faculty agreed, provided there were no changes to the campus, and one of IU's few professors, Theophilus Wylie—the half cousin of then–IU president Andrew Wylie—was charged with overseeing the effort.

There were more restrictions. The team, which called itself the University Baseball Club, would not be allowed to leave Bloomington to play what were described as "match" games. The team was also denied the opportunity to play an out-of-town team after all arrangements had already been made for the game. The challenged team wanted a new baseball in return for the game, and the team believed the school should pay for it. After some discussion, the faculty came up with a ball, but the captain of the opposing team refused to accept it, and the game was canceled.

The bottom line is that the faculty members weren't all that thrilled about the game showing up on campus. Twineham wrote in the same *"I" Men* issue: "The faculties of the various colleges in Indiana in those days were by no means baseball enthusiasts; they were fearful lest we give too much time to the sport and neglect the more serious work of college life."

Twineham also remembered McDonald "getting sent home" for playing a midweek game in Terre Haute.

Baseball was far from the organized ritual it would come to be. That first Indiana University team didn't have a planned schedule. There were some scrimmages against other colleges, but they weren't official games. IU played local town teams, high school teams, or players who worked at a local factory.

It was all just for the fun of the game. There were no uniforms or gloves, and the school didn't support the team in any way.

But the players remembered each other well.

According to McDonald, McIntire, the catcher, "displayed more grit and nerve behind the bat than anyone." McIntire didn't have any protection of any kind save for a pair of high-topped boots with his pants stuffed in the top. When it came time to bat, McIntire would take off his boots and run the bases in his socks.

"He was a corker," McDonald wrote.

Rice was described in the classic good-field, no-hit fashion.

"Rice at short was a good player, stockily built, and while not being a long batter, was to be relied upon in the pinches," McDonald said.

The *Indiana Student*—the brand-new student newspaper in its first volume, which would undergo a number of name changes before eventually becoming the *Indiana Daily Student* (note: references to the student newspaper will be era appropriate throughout this book)—took notice of the team on campus, writing in its May 17, 1867, edition under the headline "Base Ball": "Strolling through the suburbs of the city a few afternoons since, our attention was attracted by a number of persons taking vigorous exercise by what appeared, to us, to be chasing butterflies; but, upon approaching them, we found it to be the university base ball club taking field exercise to the tune of double-quick. This club has been in existence but a short time, yet some of them think themselves perfect in the art."

Showcasing the overall ignorance surrounding the game, a newspaper reporter asked one of the players "what degree of proficiency" they had attained, and he received a nonsensical answer: "He replied that they had just received the thirty-third degree, and, on their own ground, could 'beat anything in the state.' (Being ignorant of the mysteries of base ballry, we asked an explanation and were informed that the thirty-third degree was the highest and most honorable, and entitled them to be dubbed 'most excellent knights of the paddle.') From what we witnessed, we feel free to say that their excellencies are second to no other club in Bloomington."

The *Indiana Student* reported that challenges had been sent to teams at Yale, Harvard, Greencastle (home of then–Indiana Asbury University, later to be renamed DePauw University), and other teams in Monroe County.

The newspaper also threw in an endorsement of the effort.

"Clubs of this kind are very conducive to the health of the students," the paper wrote. "We would be glad to see more of them."

A couple of weeks later—June 7, to be exact—the *Indiana Student* tried to stir the pot some more with regard to challenging other teams, writing, "We will cheerfully acknowledge that the Yale club can beat anything in existence, that the Harvard club has been beaten, that the Amherst club is the best in the U.S., and the University club can best any of them."

As the games weren't exactly official, and records weren't anywhere near a priority, there are no results of games from this era. Indiana's first team also proved to be short-lived. McDonald served as captain in both 1866 and 1867 for the unofficial team, but in 1868 and 1869, there is no record of a captain for the squad.

Bynum commented in the *"I" Men's Notes* that "there was not much playing of baseball during the years of 1868 and 1869. Mr. McDonald was the prime mover, and after he left college, the club did not do much playing while I was in Bloomington."

This begs the question: What happened?

McDonald is listed in multiple twentieth-century sources as an 1870 graduate of IU, but in the extremely thorough Annual Reports of Indiana University for 1867–69; 70–75, McDonald disappears following his sophomore year, and he is never listed as an alumnus of the university.

In other words, the guy credited as the "father of IU baseball" apparently never graduated from IU. And when he left after his sophomore year, baseball disappeared from the campus, too.

It would return in 1870 when Twineham took up the captaincy, but the team devolved into an intramural entity throughout the 1870s, with a number of teams organizing on campus. The university wouldn't come together to field an official team again until the early 1880s.

That first IU team, incidentally, turned out to be a collection of "who's who in the state of Indiana" over the following half century. Maxwell became a doctor. Bynum became a state representative from Indianapolis and later a US Congressman. A six-footer, Bynum cut an impressive figure, one that wasn't easily intimidated. In May 1890, Bynum was censured by the Republican-led House of Representatives for calling a Republican foe a tyrant and despot. He was accused of "unparliamentary language," and when he was brought to the floor of the House to face the music, the entire contingent of the Democratic party came down to join him in the well as a show of support.

Hall, meanwhile, was elected lieutenant governor of the state of Indiana. Jones, Twineham, and Bothwell became well-known lawyers, while Howe became a prominent contractor in Southern California. Nave was a banker and a large landowner in Attica, Indiana, and McDonald became the general manager of three different railroads before heading into a life of farming.

McDonald was awarded the first "I" Man letter in the organization's history in 1899, and he was an active member of the "I" Men until his passing. He was even part of a group of four players, along with Bynum, Twineham, and Hall, who celebrated the founding of the team by attending the October 30, 1915, IU football game at Washington Ball Park in Indianapolis.

McDonald was one of seven living players at that game, and he would pass away following complications from surgery following a bout of pneumonia January 28, 1919.

Jones—the youngest of the original team members—died at age seventy-four in February 1926. His passing was noted in the February 13 edition of *The Indiana Alumnus* under the headline "Father of Diamond Game Here Is Dead."

> Aquilla Q. Jones, who died Sunday at Indianapolis, and who was a former student at Indiana University, was known widely among IU alumni as the "father of baseball" at Indiana University.
>
> "I am very sorry to hear of the death of Aquilla Q. Jones," said President William L. Bryan. "An interesting episode in his life was his introduction of the great game of baseball into Indiana and into Indiana University."

> Mr. Jones came to the University in the late 60's and is said to have brought in the first baseball outfit ever possessed on campus. He organized a team and played as pitcher and had a record of winning practically all his games. He was the last survivor of Indiana University's first baseball team.

So who is the actual "father of IU baseball"? The two likely go hand in hand. McDonald and Jones knew each other when they were young, they came to IU at the same time, and they were certainly both part of the first team. McDonald, however, was actually enrolled in the university, whereas Jones was only part of the Preparatory Department.

So, technically, if one had to decide between the two, McDonald might get a slight nod. Whoever was the "father" of the game at IU, the entire team served as pioneers for athletics at the university. Intercollegiate athletics, however, would have to wait a few more years.

Baseball was played on campus on and off throughout the 1870s, but there wasn't a lot of organization. That all changed in the early 1880s.

A team was organized in 1881 and 1882, and both of those years saw games played the way they had been played in the past, taking on local town or factory teams. In 1882, the team played one game against a team from Bedford.

But in May 1883, IU athletics took its first real step into the future when it scheduled its first battle against another college team. On May 12 of that year, IU took on the team from Indiana Asbury University in nearby Greencastle on the same Seminary Square field originally created for the team sixteen years earlier.

Not that the event was highly anticipated. The *Indiana Student* sent a reporter who clearly didn't know what was going on.

"Match Game of Base Ball Between the Asbury and Indiana Universities' Nines" read a subtle headline in a mid-May edition. The reporter then did a less-than-stellar job of informing his readers about what happened.

> The *Student*'s unsophisticated reporter now realizes the immeasurable distance that lies between its own unpracticed pen and the keen classical pencil of the regular newspaper man. The match game of ball between the Greencastle and Bloomington clubs on the 12th of May caused us to know "how sharper than a serpent's tooth it is" not to be on terms of affable familiarity with the slang of the diamond.

> In default of this accomplishment, and being unable to secure the services of a professional artist in adjectives, we venture to say in our own poor way that nine gentlemanly men from Asbury clad in neat white uniforms met a hastily collected club of our boys in the campus, and beat them twenty-three to six. For five innings the team was about even—finely played on both sides and intensely interesting. At that point, T. W. Wilson's hands were so bruised that he was compelled to change from the catcher's place to the right field, and the strong point of the home club was broken as no one else was quite equal to the task of stopping balls that came from center.
>
> It might be further explained that the Bloomingtons were entirely without practice, but we only care to say that it was a gentlemanly game, well and fairly played. We should be glad, if it were possible, to give honorable mention to the numerous fine plays.

Indiana athletics had begun with a loss, but the result wasn't as important as the fact it finally gave the teams something to play for. The baseball team reconvened in the fall of 1883, with Thomas Wilson—the catcher who couldn't continue in that first game—taking over as captain for the next two years.

Records continued to be spotty for the team until the mid-1890s, but a highlight of the prerecord time period is IU's May 30, 1892, win over DePauw at the Seminary Square field—which had been named IU Athletic Park—that would decide what was called the InterCollegiate Championship Series of 1892.

On the back of a photo in the IU Archives, it is written, "There was an enormous crowd and wild excitement. 300 DePauw students went down to witness the game, and both sides were determined to win. Indiana University won the game with a score of 13 to 11. This gave her the pennant of 1892."

IU athletics were here to stay. In fact, a few miles away from where the IU-DePauw game was being played, tangible proof of Indiana's dedication to athletics would soon rise from the ground.

First, we have to go back a couple of years. During the 1888–89 school year, IU's enrollment had exploded to 321 students, more than double what it had been twenty years earlier. The university itself was a much different entity than it had been even ten years earlier, thanks to a fire that reshaped the history of IU.

Thursday, July 12, 1883, was a stormy day, and a heavy rain fell on Bloomington throughout the evening. At 10:30 p.m., lightning struck the ground and followed a telegraph wire into the room of Professor Wylie in the New College Building (also known as the Science Hall), which had been built in 1873; that set the internal framing on fire.

By the time the fire was discovered, it was already burning out of control. Despite the best efforts of the Bloomington Fire Department's new steam engine, within two hours the roof of the three-story building had collapsed. A library containing fourteen thousand volumes was destroyed, and other valuable collections suffered the wrath of the flames.

The campus was in shambles, and nobody was certain about the future of IU. There were calls for the university to move to the bigger city of Indianapolis and reestablish itself there. The board of trustees wasn't having it, and on July 24, it resolved to rebuild in Bloomington.

But that didn't mean IU had to rebuild in the same spot.

In late August, the board decided the fire was an act of God and a sign that IU should take the opportunity to expand in ways that weren't practical on the Seminary Square campus. The decision was made to buy a twenty-acre tract of woods from Moses Dunn, providing a new, expanded area for the campus to grow east of downtown Bloomington.

Buildings quickly sprang up throughout the mid-1880s, giving the campus a vibrant feel.

Meanwhile, back on the Seminary Square campus, the baseball team was getting some company. Football at IU was officially introduced on campus by Professor A. B. Woodford in 1886 by adding two players to the baseball team, and the team would play baseball and football on the same road trip (look to chapter 2 for more on the founding of the football program).

The influx of students led to a desire to create a gymnasium—two, actually: one for men, one for women—that could serve the physical needs of the students. During 1887, students complained to the board of trustees that their requests for a gymnasium had been ignored, and they cited the lack of a gym as the reason the baseball and football teams weren't more successful. After all, weren't IU men just as good as, if not better than, students at Yale, then one of the top athletic colleges in the land?

The difference was that Yale had a place to practice indoors and could separate its baseball and football seasons, thanks to the facilities. IU, meanwhile, couldn't drum up enough support for the football team to put together enough players to have a full eleven-on-eleven practice, which handicapped the team. A gymnasium would allow IU to push its athletics to new heights.

In the meantime, IU students loved to come out to cheer on their teams, and the graduating class of 1888 decided it needed some way to bond the students to the school and show its support through colors. The *Indiana Student* announced in December 1887 that the university's colors were crimson and black. The class of '88, meanwhile, had chosen colors of crimson and gold for an annual that would be published to commemorate the class.

The November 13, 1903, *Daily Student* reported, "Seniors in 1888, confronted with the problem of selecting binding colors for their annual, mixed the class and university colors to produce the cream and crimson combination. There had been no official university colors, so the Class of '88, thirty-nine in number, met to decide what Indiana's future colors would be. The cream and crimson were chosen without a dissenting vote."

IU now had a baseball team, a football team, and official university colors. But the gymnasium problem had yet to be solved. In May 1889, Dr. James D. Maxwell, an 1833 graduate of IU who had recently retired to give his full attention to his longtime duty as a trustee at Indiana University, decided to contact some colleagues about the practicality of building a gymnasium on the IU campus.

Maxwell sent a letter to Dudley Allen Sargent of Harvard College, one of the leaders of the physical fitness movement in the United States and later the founder of the Sargent Normal School of Physical Training. Sargent responded to Maxwell on May 22 with the following letter:

> Dear Sir:
>
> Your letter of May 18th is at hand. I send you by the same that takes this letter a copy of the reformed Physical Training that was (approved) by the Bureau of Education at Washington two or three years since. It contains more general information on the subject of gymnasiums than I could possibly give you in any other enumeration.
>
> I send you enclosed a rough sketch of the best plan of building a large, serviceable, yet cheaply constructed gymnasium. Such a building with a basement, bathing facilities, dressing room lockers and equipment for gymnasium could be made for $15,000 of brick. I'd argue to be made for less, if constructed wholly of

wood. Fifteen hundred dollars would secure you a first-class equipment for such a gymnasium. Perhaps a similar structure to the one I have drafted might be made. The principle thing is to keep to the regulation health for the cross beams (20 to 22 feet) and 12 ft. for the height under the running track, with 10 or 12 ft. for the basement. If you could build up the roof as indicated by the dotted lines, it would offer you better light and air, and consequently better ventilation.

If you could have the bath rooms and dressing locker arranged in your basement as indicated in the plans for Lehigh University, it would be an economical one, though it would be better in many respects in sections. There is an increasing tendency to do away with the tub bath in the gymnasium, and confine the bathing to showers and sponge baths. This necessitates a room (12 × 12) so constructed that water will do no damage and drain off rapidly after it has been used. Do not have any plaster in the gymnasium. Have as much light and air as you can get and let it come from above. If I can give you any further information please let me hear from you.

Very truly yours, D.A. Sargent

Shortly after receiving Sargent's letter, Maxwell contacted William Gay Ballantine, a former Greek professor at IU and a professor of Greek at Oberlin College in Ohio, about the gym. William was the son of Elisha Ballantine, a professor at IU and onetime vice-president of Indiana University who would go on to have a building named after him on campus.

Ballantine forwarded Maxwell's letter to F. F. Jewett, a chemistry teacher at Oberlin and a member of the advisory committee for the Oberlin board of trustees. Jewett would mentor a student named Charles Martin Hall, who would go on to perfect a process for extracting aluminum for commercial use and later become the vice president of the Aluminum Company of America (Alcoa). Hall's process eventually would lead to the widespread use of aluminum alloys, which is presently used to construct stadium seating . . . but we're getting off track.

On June 1, Jewett answered Maxwell's questions about the gymnasium with the following letter:

Dear Sir,

Your letter of May 31st to Prof. Ballantine was handed to me as chairman of the gymnasium committee for reply. We have connected with the college two gymnasiums, one for the young men and one for the ladies, both of which are tolerably well equipped with apparatus. Our young men's gymnasium is a wooden

> structure, one story high without basement and heated by two stoves. I do not remember the size exactly but I would think it must be 75 by 35 or 40 feet. One end of it is partitioned off for a dressing room, provided with rows of lockers two high for holding the clothing of the students.
>
> Each locker has a lock and key, so that each student can keep his things safely. The main room will accommodate on the floor about thirty-five students, not more than that conveniently. We have dumb bells, Indian clubs, and such apparatus sufficient for that number of students, but of chest weights about twelve.
>
> Our young man has charge of the whole. He had special training in gymnastics having studied under Dr. Luther H. Gulick who has charge of the Gymnastic Department of the YMCA Training School for Christian Workers at Springfield, Mass. He teaches one or two classes a day himself and then has students who he has trained take charge of the other classes. There are seven classes, not organized according to proficiency but according to the time they can best devote to physical practice. The members of our preparatory dept. are all obliged to attend daily, but with the college students, it is optional whether they go or not. If our building was large enough to accommodate classes of twice the size, we should require attendance from all. The building did not cost over $2,000, and the apparatus in it I should think could be purchased for four or five hundred. I should have said in regard to the director of the gymnasium that the college pays him $35 a month, and the other teachers (students) fifteen cents an hour.

(Fun facts: Jewett mentions that they have a young man in charge of physical education who studied under Dr. Luther H. Gulick at the YMCA in Springfield, Massachusetts. Gulick previously studied physical education under Sargent and would later become the head of physical education at the Springfield YMCA. It was Gulick who, in 1891, ordered one of his instructors, James Naismith, to come up with a game that would not take up much room and help the men stay in shape during the long New England winter. Naismith, of course, came up with a game called "basket-ball," which people from Indiana would come to enjoy tremendously.)

Despite all of Maxwell's legwork on the gym, the university didn't act on constructing a gym right away. Two full years later, IU still didn't have a gymnasium.

But that was about to change.

During a November 7, 1891, meeting of the IU board of trustees, the following motion was passed authorizing the construction of a gymnasium on campus.

"On the motion of Mr. Youche, the Local Executive Committee and with the concurrence of the President of the University, we're authorized and directed to construct and equip on the campus a gymnasium for the use of young men at a cost not to exceed $1,000.00 which sum was ordered appropriated out of the contingent fund of the university."

The public was notified three days later. Wedged between a note that "Miss Fan Watson has been enjoying a very pleasant visit for the last three days from her sister" and an item reporting that the IU football team had lost a practice game to Butler 28–6, the November 10, 1891, *Bloomington Telephone* printed the de facto birth announcement.

"It will be noted in the report of the meeting of the Board of Trustees that the I.U. is to have a regular gymnasium," the paper reported. "It will be a frame structure, located north of Owen Hall, and will be so constructed that it can be improved upon as fast as the means are provided. Work will begin as soon as practicable. Athletics are certainly on the rise at I.U."

Although the IU baseball and football teams had been around for a while, there had never been a dedicated athletic facility on the new campus at IU. The gymnasium was built seventy-one feet north and four feet east of the west edge of Owen Hall. The building was designed to accommodate additions, including a running track and bathing facilities. Once construction began, the work moved quickly.

The December 8, 1891, edition of the *Telephone* reported, "The gymnasium will be a frame structure 50 feet wide, 66-feet long and with 18 feet ceiling. Work is progressing rapidly, and as there is no plastering to be done, the building can be finished without delay."

Just over a month later, the *Telephone* announced that "the gymnasium building is about completed and will soon be ready for the apparatus. As there is only a small amount [of money] left for equipment, the apparatus will not be very extensive at first but will be ample for our present needs. Additions will be made as needed."

On January 22, 1892, the gymnasium was dedicated during IU's seventy-second Foundation Day festivities. At 2:00 p.m., the public was invited to see the new facility. Following a short address by Professor Ernest Huffcut, the master of ceremonies for the day, a display of gymnastic exercises were performed by the ladies' gymnastic drill, led by Mrs. Harriet Colburn Sanderson. The ladies marched, performed "Swedish exercises," and worked with "chest weights." The men's gymnastics exercises were omitted because the apparatus had not yet arrived, but the *Telephone* reported that "the performers gave evidence of excellent training."

The university imposed a one-dollar fee per term on students for using the gymnasium. The fee was justified by two reasons. The *Telephone* reported that "those who are not in earnest will not care to throw away the dollar for nothing, and this will keep a great many stragglers out of the way of the others who mean business." Secondly, the money would be used to buy new apparatus and equipment for the gymnasium.

The gym was a hit. By mid-February, the apparatus for the building had arrived, and more than fifty students—at a time when roughly four hundred students were enrolled—were taking part in training. Gymnastics became one of the most popular classes on campus, with practice running from 3:00 to 4:00 p.m. and classes being taught from 4:00 to 5:00 p.m. The football and baseball teams used the facility as well, and students could make use of the horizontal bars, parallel bars, Indian clubs, chest weights, ladders, and vaulting bars as long as they had paid their one dollar and had a pair of "solid rubber shoes."

By December 1892, the Trustees approved another $150 for apparatus for the gym, and a twelve-foot by thirty-foot dressing/locker room was approved. The addition was finished by January 1893, and that month's edition of the *Indiana Student* reported that "a great deal of new apparatus has been added to the gymnasium."

The facility was undoubtedly popular, but its small size—it was more like a barn than anything else—quickly became a problem on a growing campus. In fact, less than a year after the gymnasium opened, it was hinted that the school may have to go another direction. The December 16, 1892, *Telephone* said the university had delivered its biennial report, and although the news was encouraging, it was clear that IU had to expand. The graduates for 1892 numbered seventy-seven, and in the previous four years, attendance had doubled. With that in mind, it was suggested that more construction would be in the offing.

"The library building, which was erected a few months ago, has had to be utilized as a class-room," IU's report said. "The school has no assembly room where the students can meet as a body."

With that sentence the seed of an idea for the construction of some sort of assembly hall was planted.

The gymnasium served its purpose as an athletic facility for four years. But in 1896, a new men's gymnasium was completed just a couple dozen yards east of the original gymnasium, the athletic equipment was moved out, and the original gym took on its new role, that of carpenter's shop. The building helped with the construction of other facilities on campus, whether athletic or otherwise, for the next thirty-six years.

It also would be the birthplace of basketball at IU, but more on that in just a bit.

The building was razed without fanfare in 1932 to allow room for a road to pass between Owen Hall and the newly constructed Indiana Memorial Union. There is no marker to commemorate IU's original gymnasium, and for decades, students have walked or driven through the spot that once focused IU on the importance of athletics.

FIGURE 1.1. Indiana University was established as the State Seminary of Indiana with one college building that later added an attached house for a single professor. *IU Archives P0022520*

FIGURE 1.2. Malcolm "Mack" McDonald has been called the "father of IU baseball," and he certainly played an important role in bringing athletics to IU. *IU Archives P0021446*

FIGURE 1.3. Four of the seven living players from the 1867 baseball team gathered for a reunion in 1915 at an IU football game. *IU Archives P0043495*

FIGURE 1.4. The Seminary Square campus as it looked in 1883. The loss of the Science Hall that same year was the catalyst for IU's move to its current campus. *IU Archives P0022545*

FIGURE 1.5. Dunn's Woods, shown here in 1891, was the perfect spot for the expansion of the IU campus and is now known as the Old Crescent of the university. *IU Archives P0022535*

FIGURE 1.6. Indiana's 1892 baseball win over DePauw on the Seminary Square campus was the university's first high-profile athletics victory. *IU Archives P0032101*

FIGURE 1.7. The original Men's Gymnasium, built in 1892 and shown here in 1918, was IU's first permanent athletic facility and was later the site of the first official basketball practice. *IU Archives P0022843*

FIGURE 1.8. The Men's Gymnasium sat just north of Owen Hall, as seen in this picture from the mid-1890s. *IU Archives P0020050*

2

The Arrival of Football and a New Home

Baseball exploded in popularity in the post–Civil War era, but it was far from the only major sport to suddenly take off.

Intercollegiate football became part of the landscape when Rutgers took on the College of New Jersey—later known as Princeton—November 6, 1869. Football looked substantially different in those days. Each team featured twenty-five players, and the object was to kick or bat the ball in the opponents' goal using their hands, feet, heads, or sides. Nobody could pick up the ball and run with it, and they certainly couldn't throw it.

It was barely football, but it's what everyone counts.

The game slowly became more refined, and it took a quantum leap October 19, 1873, when representatives from Yale, Columbia, Princeton, and Rutgers met at the Fifth Avenue Hotel in New York to establish a set of rules to govern the game. A total of twelve rules were created.

1. The ground shall be 400 feet long and 250 feet broad.
2. The distance between the posts of each goal shall be 25 feet.
3. The number for match games shall be 20 to a side.
4. To win a game 6 goals are necessary, but that side shall be considered victorious which, when the game is called, shall have scored

the greatest number of goals, provided that number be 2 or more. To secure a goal the ball must pass between the posts.
5. No player shall throw or carry the ball. Any violation of this regulation shall constitute a foul, and the player so offending shall throw the ball perpendicularly into the air to a height of at least 12 feet and the ball shall not be in play until it has touched the ground.
6. When the ball passes out of bounds it is a foul, and the player causing it shall advance at right angles to the boundary line, 15 paces from the point where the ball went, and shall proceed as in rule 5.
7. No tripping shall be allowed, nor shall any player use his hands to hold or push an adversary.
8. The winner of the toss shall have the choice of the first goal, and the sides shall change goals after every successive inning. In starting the ball it shall be fairly kicked, not "babied," from a point 150 feet in front of the starter's goal.
9. Until the ball is kicked no player on either side shall be in advance of a line parallel to the line of his goal and distant from it 150 feet.
10. There shall be two judges, one from each of the contesting colleges, and one referee; all to be chosen by the captains.
11. No player shall wear spikes or iron plates upon his shoes.
12. In all matches a No. 6 ball shall be used, furnished by the challenging side and to become the property of the victor.

The rules were refined in 1876, and the Intercollegiate Football Association was established. In the late 1870s and early 1880s, rules proposed by Yale captain Walter Camp, later to be known as the "father of American football," were introduced to create a game that looked more like what we've come to know. The game continued to be tweaked over time, with the addition of downs and a line of scrimmage in 1882, and scoring rules were tweaked in 1883.

Arthur Woodford, meanwhile, played football for Yale and graduated from the school's Sheffield Scientific School in 1881. He came to Bloomington in 1885 as a professor of economics. Considering the popularity of the game on the East Coast, Woodford was somewhat surprised to find that IU didn't have a football team and that, in fact, there wasn't a lot of interest in the sport.

He set out to rectify the situation by going after people who had already shown a willingness to enjoy the frivolities of sports—the baseball team. Woodford recruited two other players to the squad, giving IU exactly eleven players, including Harry Wise. Wise is listed as a captain for the team, but there is no record of games being played, and games were likely played more as an activity than as an organized game.

The team was recognized more formally in 1886, but it wasn't until October 25, 1887, that IU football played its first official game. The team went on the road to play DePauw in baseball before taking on Franklin College in Indianapolis.

Thomas Clarks' *Indiana University: Midwest Pioneer* described the game.

"The first football players wore tight-fitting white canvas suits," Clark wrote. "Shirts were laced up the front, and some of the players cut blades from broad grain scoops and strapped them over their chests."

Franklin won 10–8, but that score is pretty impressive when you consider the following two facts. First, Indiana brought just twelve players to the game, which meant there was only one substitute. They didn't bring more players because it was reported that they didn't realize football was going to be such a physical game, which is odd considering the game had already been played on campus for two years, and Woodford was a former college player. Second, the team didn't bother to practice before the Franklin game because it was too busy with the baseball season, so IU was unprepared to play.

It was the only game IU played that season, but Indiana football had begun.

In what would become a trend, the football team struggled in those early years. Records show a single tie against DePauw in 1888, and the team went 0–2 in 1889. No games were played during the 1890 season, and IU lost its first five games of the 1891 season.

It wasn't until IU took on the Louisville Athletic Club in the last game of the 1892 season that the team finally scored its first victory. The game was a 30–0 rout and was the only victory in coach Billy Herod's career.

The 1893 season saw IU football go 1–4–1, but wins and losses aren't the takeaway from that season. The key was the presence of a player who would help establish IU's reputation as being an open environment for minority athletes.

Preston Eagleson arrived at IU in the fall of 1893 looking to earn a degree as an educator, and he took the opportunity to push himself as a halfback on the football team. There wasn't an official coach of the team following Herod's departure in 1891, but Eagleson was welcomed onto the ball club and spent three seasons on the gridiron in Bloomington.

He earned his bachelor's degree in 1896, becoming the second African American to graduate from Indiana, and he became a teacher. He later became the first African American to earn a master's degree from IU, picking up an MA in philosophy in 1906.

As records of the time are nonexistent outside of results, it's impossible to know the impact Eagleson had on the budding program. Still, during a time of less-than-enthusiastic support for racial minorities in the United States, Eagleson's presence and acceptance on the team is a sign that at least some in Bloomington were willing to keep an open mind for a little while.

Eagleson would be the only African American player at IU until the early 1930s, and he passed away in 1911 at the age of thirty-three. African Americans, meanwhile, found obstacles in their way following Eagleson's time on the team. In fact, an unofficial "University Team" existed in the 1910s that was called the "colored eleven" by local newspapers, showing that although African Americans played football at IU, they did so outside of the official IU team.

Eagleson walked away from the gridiron before the 1896 season, and in September of that year, IU hired Madison G. Gonterman, formerly of the athletics department at Harvard, as the new head football coach. Students had handled the job over the previous few years, and Gonterman brought more authority, discipline, and organization to the game.

Gonterman came to IU and took a look at the IU Athletic Park, and he declared that IU needed to build a more substantial athletics grounds than the remnants of a thirty-year-old makeshift field on the Seminary Square campus. Gonterman wanted a cinder track installed to aid with the athletics program, but IU didn't have the room on its campus for the kind of facility Gonterman was asking for. Indiana would ultimately deliver Gonterman's wish, but it wouldn't be until after he was gone.

Indiana needed more land, and whenever Indiana needed land during the late nineteenth and early twentieth centuries, it turned to Moses Dunn.

The July 9, 1897, edition of the *Bloomington Telephone* reported that the university had purchased fourteen lots that had been a part of the Dunn Farm, extending from Third Street to the creek that ran near the Dunn Cemetery.

"[The university] is expected to sell all the lots within a short time," the *Telephone* reported. "They will largely be the property of members of the University faculty and substantial and attractive residences will be constructed. Among those who have already purchased lots are Dr. Swain, Profs. Rogers, Bergstrom, Fetter and Rhetts, and Judge Reinhard and Theodore Louden."

The paper, however, was wrong, and IU wasn't about to build a late-1800s version of a subdivision so close to campus.

IU president Joseph Swain informed the board of trustees on November 1, 1897, that the way had been cleared for construction for a new playing field for football and baseball, and grading needed to begin for the running track and possible tennis courts.

Professor John F. Newsome, a teacher in the Department of Geology, was placed in charge of building the new field. He selected a site east of the current Memorial Union, just down the hill from the new Men's Gymnasium. The administration, however, wasn't about to allow good materials go to waste now that it was leaving the IU Athletic Park.

The August 24, 1897, edition of the *Telephone* reported that the "fence around the base ball park at the old college campus has been removed and will be placed around the new Alumni field at the new college. Prof. Roy Perring has charge and states that the work of grading the new field will commence about Sept. 1st."

Grading the new field took a lot of work. For instance, Spanker's Branch was an issue. The creek ran right through the area that was proposed to house the new athletic grounds, and before the fields could be used, Spanker's Branch had to be diverted to the south. Spanker's Branch, by the way, would eventually receive a different name. During a trip back to IU after taking over as president at Stanford, former IU president David Starr Jordan told a group of students at the university chapel that he didn't have ambitions to have a building on the Bloomington campus named after him. Instead, he hoped Spanker's Branch would someday be named after him.

From that point on, Spanker's Branch was known as the Jordan River.

(Fun fact: As workers began to relocate Spanker's Branch, the university started to dig a deep well to furnish drinking water to the new campus. The well, which would be more than ninety feet deep when completed, would eventually be covered by the Rose Well House, a gift in 1908 from alumnus Theodore F. Rose. The Rose Well House was constructed using the portals of the Old College building, which had been a part of the Seminary Square campus. After the campus moved to its current location, the Old College building was sold to the Bloomington School Board to be used as a high school. The portals are one of the few remnants of the Seminary Square campus to make their way to the current IU campus.)

The new athletic field was ready for use during the fall of 1897. The Hoosier football squad was the first to use the nameless facility, battling Rose Polytechnic (which would later become the Rose-Hulman Institute of Technology) to a 6–6 tie. A two-plank board fence was the only seating in place at the time, and seats for the game were free. Indiana went 6–1–1 on the season, beating such powerhouses as Bedford, the Indianapolis Manual Training School, and DePauw along the way.

After going 12–3–1 in two seasons as IU's football coach, Gonterman moved on. He had been taking law classes at IU, and he returned to Harvard to finish his law degree. He would be replaced by James H. Horne, one of the critical characters in Indiana's early athletics history.

Simply put, James Horne is the unsung hero of Indiana athletics. Without his guidance in the late nineteenth and early twentieth century, IU's history might be drastically different.

Born July 24, 1874, James Howard Horne grew up in New Hampshire and graduated in 1897 from Bowdoin College. There, he spent time as the assistant director of gymnasium, and when Gonterman left IU to return to law school, Horne took over Gonterman's official job, that of director of gymnasium (think of it as a precursor to director of athletics).

Horne took over as the coach of the football team, leading Indiana to a 10–3–2 record in his first two seasons. He also spent two seasons as the baseball coach, and he went down in history as the first basketball coach of Indiana University. We'll have more about that saga in chapter 3, but Horne was critically influential in leading IU into the future during a turbulent time.

Whereas faculty members were concerned about the time being devoted to baseball in the 1860s, by the late 1890s, university presidents were acknowledging the recognition athletics could bring to their schools.

In January 1895, Purdue president James Smart met with seven other university presidents at the Palmer House in Chicago to create a set of rules that could govern an intercollegiate association and keep their individual athletic programs from descending into chaos. College sports were becoming ever more popular, and there was a struggle between academics and the athletic-minded factions over the role of sports.

Among those principles were rules to restrict eligibility to actual, full-time college students in good academic standing, eliminating the encroachment of paid ringers in the college game. Other rules focused on the appointment of responsible and university-controlled athletic committees, while still others aimed to make the game safer.

A year later, on February 8, 1896, one faculty member each from Purdue, Illinois, Wisconsin, Chicago, Minnesota, Northwestern, and Michigan met at the Palmer House in Chicago and agreed to officially form the Western Conference.

Four years later, IU president Joseph Swain convinced the board of trustees to vote to join the Western Conference along with the University of Iowa, creating what quickly became known as the Big Nine.

Baseball finally got a chance to play on the field in the spring of 1898. A diamond was laid out on the football field, and IU celebrated the opportunity to play in better conditions than were afforded by the University Athletic Field. Unfortunately, there was the problem of the Jordan River. When the river was diverted, no effort was made to try to improve drainage on the field. When the spring rains came, they not only soaked the ground from above, but the water from the river would also seep into the ground, making the entire area a muddy mess for weeks afterward.

It was during this time that the facility was finally named Jordan Field for its proximity to the Jordan River and in honor of Jordan himself. The football team made the most of its home-field advantage, despite not playing in front of large crowds during the early days. A number of contemporary stories say Indiana didn't allow an opponent to score a point at Jordan Field during the 1898, 1899, and 1900 seasons (IU's record book shows that some teams may have scored in games, but those could have come during neutral site games that weren't designated as such in the record book. When in doubt, it's a good idea to take the word of the people who were there).

IU played its first games in what would become the Big Ten at Jordan Field in 1900. Indiana and Iowa joined what had been known as the Western Conference in 1899, and they became a part of the newly named Big Nine the following year. The Big Nine wouldn't become known as the Big Ten until the 1917 season when Michigan—which had earlier been a member of the conference before dropping out for nine years—rejoined the league. The conference dropped back to the Big Nine during the 1940s when the University of Chicago dropped out, but it returned to Big Ten status in 1950 when Michigan State was added to the league.

But we're getting off track.

The baseball team, nicknamed the "Crimson"—the more familiar nickname wouldn't come for a few decades—struggled to find success on its new field, hovering around the .500 mark for the early part of the first decade of the twentieth century. It wasn't exactly as if the Crimson were playing in the lap of luxury at the field. The field featured no dugouts—just benches—and the dimensions were cozy. Although no official measurements remain, Ernie Andres, a former IU baseball coach who played at Jordan Field from 1937 to 1939, remembered in a document in the IU archives that right field couldn't have been more than 250 feet, center field was believed to be about 360 feet and left field was estimated to be 330 feet. A fence surrounded the complex, and the edges of the field were graded upward, both serving as a warning track and turning the area into a bowl.

The board of trustees, meanwhile, worked to improve the conditions on the field. A sum of $500 was appropriated in 1901 to construct bleachers to finally provide some seating. In June of 1902, money was allocated to grade the ground in the northeast corner of the field, and tile drainage was finally to be laid. Surface drainage was to be added where practical, and it was ordered that the fence surrounding the field should be rebuilt.

One of the interesting features of the field was the presence of Dunn Cemetery, which was—and still is—situated just across the Jordan River from the field. It is known as God's Acre because it was deeded to the Dunn family in perpetuity and can never be legally taken over by the university, despite the fact IU completely surrounds the cemetery, and it served as an interesting background during a baseball game in the early 1900s.

With the Crimson in the middle of what was described in the *Daily Student* as a heated game, a funeral procession descended on the cemetery, which is reserved for descendants of Elinor Dunn, Agnes Alexander, and Jennet Irwin—three sisters who were heroines of the Revolutionary War. The game was stopped; the men removed their hats, and everybody waited until the ceremony concluded. Then it was "Play ball!"

Horne spent the fall of 1900 and the spring of 1901 working on establishing a new "basket ball" team at Indiana, and he led the Crimson to a 1–3 record that first season. The basketball team was a nice diversion for Horne, but he knew the Crimson needed to continue to improve its football team if he were to hold on to his job for the future.

IU opened the season with a 24–6 win over Wabash September 28, and it followed a week later with a 57–0 pounding of Rose Polytechnic. Because touchdowns were worth five points back then, IU actually scored ten TDs on the day and converted just seven of ten extra points. A crowd of 180 was on hand at Jordan Field to watch the Crimson, and Horne believed his team could have played better despite the blowout score.

The next week, Indiana's offense failed it on a trip to Michigan, and the Crimson lost 33–0 to the Wolverines in front of a crowd of two thousand. Not that IU was alone. The 1901 Michigan squad finished the season 11–0 and outscored its opponents 550–0. The Wolverines finished the season with a 49–0 win over Stanford in the Rose Bowl, the first bowl game ever played. IU was outweighed by at least twenty pounds at nearly every position, and the general consensus seemed to be that the Crimson were just lucky to get out of Ann Arbor without suffering any major injuries.

The next big game would come two weeks later against Purdue, and the team would be getting some help with the addition of assistant coach and former Harvard star Everetts Wrenn to the staff. Wrenn had helped Indiana prepare for the Boilermakers during the 1900 season, and his arrival would be met with great fanfare.

But first, Indiana had one more opponent to battle before the showdown with Purdue. Franklin would be coming to Jordan Field on October 19, and IU hoped it could get back on the winning track.

To a certain extent it is at this point that the fog of time descends on our story. Copies of the *Daily Student* from the time period of the game no longer exist thanks to a fire, and it is that resource that is most detailed when it comes to Hoosier athletics from this time period. The good news is the city of Bloomington featured other resources, including the *Bloomington World* and the *Bloomington Courier*, two papers that seemed to be partners at the time. The October 19 edition of the *World* listed the starting lineups for both teams, but its coverage of the Franklin game fell to the *Courier*.

Unlike many other games of the time, play-by-play of this battle doesn't exist. Still, IU came out of the gates and dominated from the opening kickoff, taking control of the game early. "Franklin did nothing more than line up against the Varsity Saturday," the October 22, 1901, *Courier* wrote. "Indiana's plays were fast, her interference excellent and her teamwork on offensive play did her great credit. Indiana made 7 touch downs in the first half, and Clevenger kicked the same number of goals. The half ended with the score 42–0."

In case you're wondering, yes, the Clevenger mentioned was Zora Clevenger, a five-foot-seven, 145-pound halfback whose college career would lead to his election to the College Football Hall of Fame in 1968. Clevenger would also coach both baseball and basketball at IU, and he served as Director of Athletics at Indiana from 1923 to 1946.

To Franklin's credit, the team didn't flee Jordan Field at halftime despite facing the massive deficit. But times didn't get better for the Fighting Baptists despite the fact IU emptied its bench in a time when substitutions were extremely rare. Horne brought in subs at the end and tackle positions, and the entire Crimson backfield was replaced with four new players (remember, folks, it was single-wing football back in those days).

"Touch downs had been made when the scrubs were put in, and Clevenger failed on one goal making the score 59–0," the *Courier* wrote. "The scrubs increased the score by 3 touchdowns, and Driesback failed to kick one goal, making the final score 76 to 0."

The *Courier* did credit Franklin with continuing to battle even as the scoreboard got out of hand.

"Franklin put up a game fight and played with a spirit that would characterize few teams playing against such odds," the paper wrote.

All told, Indiana scored thirteen touchdowns on the day, and the Crimson converted eleven of thirteen extra-point attempts. No real stats were kept at the time, so there's no record of IU's total offense, rushing yards, or any other modern stats.

As it turned out, Indiana's record-setting output wasn't a cause for celebration. The newspapers quickly pivoted to the IU-Purdue game, and the Franklin game slipped into the past. By the next spring, it was almost completely forgotten. The game is listed in the 1902 *Arbutus* under IU's schedule, but not a word about the game is written, the focus being on the Purdue game.

Indiana split the rest of its games during the second half of the season, losing during trips to Illinois and Notre Dame while picking up wins at Ohio State and at home against DePauw. Indiana closed out the season with a 6–3 record overall and a 1–2 record in the Western Conference. Horne would remain as head coach for three more seasons, and Clevenger went on to the career described above. The team would reunite from time to time, but the focus was never on that spectacular outing against Franklin. That game was virtually hidden in the record books until Kevin Wilson and the 2013 IU football team scored seventy-three points in a win over Indiana State to shine a spotlight on what proved to be Indiana's most prolific offensive day in history.

Despite the efforts of the trustees to try to improve Jordan Field, students still complained about conditions at Jordan Field. A letter from someone identified as "Knocker" appeared in the May 25, 1904, edition of the *Daily Student* whining about the difficulty getting to games.

"Why doesn't the University, the Athletic Association or someone repair the driveway leading to Jordan Field?" Knocker asked. "Many people prefer to attend the games in carriages and to do so at present necessitates going hub-deep in mud. It is not customary to attend games in log wagons nor to wear overalls, but nothing better can at present go over the driveway without damage."

A running track and field equipment were added to Jordan Field in time for IU's outdoor track season in 1904, but the rain was a constant problem. By 1905, students were starting to get restless with the state of moisture on the field. Despite the efforts to drain the field, the *Daily Student* complained that the complex wasn't up to standards of the day and should be moved.

The April 28, 1905, edition of the *Daily Student* reported:

> At noon yesterday the regular diamonds on Jordan Field was so heavy and soggy that it was found impossible to play the game there.... A force of men was set to work to change the location of the parallelogram for the game with Ohio State. Jordan Field, while all right in dry weather, is a source of continuous annoyance in wet. The field is low and has practically no drainage facilities. A heavy rain soaks it through and through, and a week's time is required for it to dry out.
>
> Noting this state of affairs an old discussion is being revised as to the advisability of changing the athletic field from its present situation to the top of Dunn's hill. Several citizens are said to have suggested this location before Jordan Field was chosen. With far less work than has taken to put Jordan Field in its present condition, an athletic field could be made on top of the hill that would be as level as the present field, and in addition would be exceptionally well drained. No ponds would stand over it in the winter, and in the spring we would not have to wait four or five weeks after the warm weather commence to begin out-of-door practice. And then with a new $75,000 stone gymnasium situated somewhere in the vicinity of the proposed field, Indiana would have no apologies to make to any university in the West.

Indiana eventually would get around to building the gymnasium, but it would be a while. Jordan Field wasn't going anywhere. In fact, the lack of drainage would become a source of great excitement in just a few years.

College life was a lot different in 1908 than it is a century later. There were no TVs, no radios, no internet, no cell phones, no keggers, no texting, none of it. Entertainment came through playing sports and going to local dances and assemblies. In the winter of late 1907 and early 1908, ice skating became a bit of a fad in the United States, and IU wasn't about to stay behind the curve on that issue. Without a natural pond anywhere near campus, the students and faculty decided they would just have to make one themselves.

In the February 8, 1908, edition of the *Daily Student*, a headline screamed, "JORDAN FIELD IS FLOODED." It stated:

> At four o'clock this afternoon, Coach Sheldon, with a force of men working under his direction, turned the hydrants on to Jordan Field and in the course of an hour the field was transformed into a veritable lake, ready for the next spell of cold weather.... As soon as the next freeze occurs, students will have the benefit of a skating resort which can be reached without the aid of a cab.

For some time there has been talk of a scheme of this kind. Jordan Field is practically useless during the winter months, and it has been felt that some advantage might be taken of the large plat of ground. Coach Sheldon has been conferring with the University officials of late and received their consent to flood Jordan Field in order that a commodious skating rink might be ready for the general enjoyment whenever the weather was cold enough to convert the watery covering into ice.

Even as football, baseball, and track and field went through their paces, Jordan Field continued its role as a multipurpose ground. The area wasn't reserved for varsity athletics, and military teams drilled on the grounds. Members of the community also made use of the field. A letter from July 5, 1907, from Alex F. Kirsch (a local businessman) to John W. Cravens (the university registrar) exists in the IU archives asking if Kirsch could use Jordan Field for the annual charity baseball game between the Clothing Clerks and the Drug Clerks in town.

By 1914, less than twenty years after the opening of the complex, students and faculty were already dreaming of bigger, better facilities for the football and baseball teams. A proposal was presented by the Department of Physical Education on June 4, 1914, to the trustees who sought to turn Jordan Field over to the department while moving the football and baseball teams east to the location near the current site of the IU Auditorium. The plan was to create a facility known as Bryan Field in honor of Indiana president William Lowe Bryan, a complex that would provide a baseball field and permanent seating in a 360-foot-by-360-foot area.

"Jordan Field does not drain well and scheduled games do not allow postponement," the Department said. "It seems economical, therefore, to plot a new 'varsity field' and turn Jordan Field over to the Department of Physical Education for general activities, which have no grounds at the present."

That plan was shot down, and a new track was built around the football field in February of 1915. The moisture on the field that spring made the use of the track a fiasco due to a lack of drainage, but it was clear Jordan Field would continue into the future as a baseball and track facility.

IU, however, had different plans when it came to football.

Remember the spot on top of Dunn's hill that was mentioned earlier? Indiana certainly noticed it, and when it came time to replace the Men's

Gymnasium, it chose that flat spot to construct the state-of-the-art facility. Included in the plans was an outdoor field that could be used until a fieldhouse was built over the spot and a better football stadium could be constructed.

Ground was broken on the new Men's Gymnasium in October of 1915, and it was fully expected that a new football field would be ready for the 1916 season. The planned final football game at Jordan Field was played against Purdue on November 20, 1915.

"Indiana University will say farewell to Jordan Field as an intercollegiate gridiron when Purdue's squad of huskies meets the crimson-clad players in the closing game of the season," the November 19, 1915, edition of the *Telephone* reported. "Next fall will find Indiana playing its intercollegiate games on the new athletic field which will be built soon just north of the present field in connection with the erection of the new $150,000 gym."

Indiana planned for a big crowd at Jordan Field and built new bleachers that could hold an extra two thousand fans on top of the existing accommodations for four thousand fans. When the dust settled, Indiana had sold more than $4,400 in tickets and set a school record for a single-game profit. IU lost 7–0, and Childs was forced out as head coach during the off-season, but the sun was undoubtedly shining on the Hoosier football program. Little did IU know that dark clouds were gathering.

With the football program finished at Jordan Field, the administration did the only thing it could at that point in the year.

It flooded the field again.

For the first time since 1908, Jordan Field would be turned into an ice-skating rink for students during the winter, but this time the rink would be run by the Memorial Union, and the process would be carefully controlled to ensure quality skating for all. Students were invited to bring their skates back with them following the Thanksgiving break, and the campus was excited about the return of skating. The December 8, 1915, *Daily Student* reported:

> All of Jordan Field, except the ball diamond, will be flooded in times of cold weather and thus covered with a thick layer of ice. It is not intended that a lake shall be made, but when cold weather comes fire hose will be used to flood the field. Each day during the cold spell more water will be added to the layer and in this way the ice will be built up to a depth of several inches.

> The plan was suggested to President Bryan by George E. Kessler, who has been employed by the University to work out a new landscape plan for the campus. Mr. Kessler said that the plan has been used successfully in playgrounds in Kansas City and other cities. No damage, he said, is done to the grass and in every way the idea is good. Snowstorms will not cheat students out of skating if the plan is carried out and the rink can be kept clean and "slick as glass" all the time.

The weather, however, didn't cooperate until January. Fluctuating temperatures frustrated students. Then equipment started breaking down. Under the baffling headline of "O Skinnay! C'Mon Over N' Go Skatin'!" the January 8, 1916, *Indiana Daily Student* reported the following:

> Latest reports from the new Union ice rink on Jordan Field, which are being watched anxiously by skating fans, assure a breathless world that the pump, which developed an acute attack of gastritis soon after it was put to work flooding the field, has full recovered and is now again on the job. The pump was placed in Jordan River Friday afternoon and had barely started operations when it became ill. An expert pump doctor was called in, who succeeded in bringing the ailing machine around overnight.
>
> At 8:30 o'clock this morning a stream of water was again playing on the field and chances for good skating soon were on the rise. After a consultation in which the best lights of the Mathematics and Physics departments were consulted, the authorities in charge of the Union's new enterprise announced that with a little good luck the rink would probably be ready today.

Despite the high hopes, the rink wouldn't actually be ready for another week. Finally, the January 14 *Indiana Daily Student* reported the good news.

"The Jordan Field ice skating rink is ready for use and was tried out this morning by a number of students," the paper reported. "The entire field has not been flooded, but at least two-thirds of it is under four inches of ice. The rink is the first to be made at Indiana University and will be run under the management of the Union." (Editor's note: The previous sentence appeared in the story, but it's just plain wrong. The same paper had reported in 1908 about a skating rink being built and used.) "An admission of ten cents will be charge in order to defray expenses. Local hardware merchants are ready to supply the demand for skates, according to their displays and announcements."

The ice remained rough for a couple of days and limited skating, and the crumbly edges of the ice created some dangerous conditions. But in those pre-litigious days, nobody seemed worried about the safety aspect of the rink, and the students and faculty got to enjoy some fun during the winter.

Unfortunately, events in the world weren't nearly as fun. The Great War, later to be renamed World War I, was raging in Europe, and the United States was doing its best to stay out of the conflict while readying its military. In addition, the United States was fighting Pancho Villa on the Mexican-American border, and IU students were entering the military to help with the fighting.

In other words, it wasn't exactly the greatest time to be building a football stadium.

The project was put on hold sometime during the spring, and the Crimson would return to Jordan Field for the time being.

In July 1916, a major change was made to Jordan Field. The baseball diamond was repositioned to help stem the tide of baseballs being lost in the Jordan River, something that had been a longtime problem. The July 16, 1916, *Indiana Daily Student* reported:

> A new baseball diamond has been laid off on Jordan Field for the baseball work of the school for high school coaches. The new baseball court faces the south bleachers instead of facing the carriage gate as formerly. The change is due to the propensity of valuable baseballs to find their way into the Jordan River or its valley and water has as baneful an influence on a baseball as the summer sun has on snow. Probably one ball a day is lost in the River. Good baseballs come at about seventy-five cents a head wholesale, and the mathematical fan can easily figure up the shrinkage.
>
> The varsity baseball team practices about five days each week for approximately twelve weeks each spring, twelve times five being sixty. Now, three-fourths of sixty is forty-five which means that about forty-five dollars worth of baseballs are lost in the season. Jordan Field has been in use since about 1897 [*sic*]. Now if the arithmetical fan will multiply forty-five by nineteen the result will be about five hundred ninety-five dollars. The little river behind the bleachers might have been covered with a portion of that fabulous sum. But the United States isn't going to fill up the Grand Canyon because a tourist tumbles in it occasionally, so roll on Jordan!

The change shifted the diamond so that the Men's Gymnasium overlooked center field, and the third-base foul line ran along the edge of the power plant that existed in the area where part of the Union now stands.

IU football returned to the field without fanfare, and the baseball team continued to plug along without any wild success. Jordan Field was used as a drill ground during World War I, and annual Armistice Day festivities were held there following the end of the conflict. The football team, meanwhile, continued to play at Jordan Field through the end of the 1923 season.

By the time the end of that year rolled around, Hoosier fans were certain that the team would be moving to a new arena. Following a drive to raise $1 million for campus improvements, including the construction of a new football stadium, work had begun on a facility along Tenth Street. The ground was excavated, and the concrete was poured, and the new stadium was a lock to be ready in time for the 1924 campaign.

But c'mon. You know things didn't go that smoothly.

Structural problems at Memorial Stadium delayed the opening and forced the Crimson to play the 1924 season as vagabonds. One home game was played in Indianapolis and another on the freshman practice field, known as Indiana Field, on the site of the current Bill Garrett Fieldhouse. Others were played at Jordan Field. IU finished 4–4 on the season and 1–3 in conference play, and the Indiana finally moved into Memorial Stadium for the 1925 season. Football may have finally been finished at Jordan Field, but the facility wasn't going anywhere.

The track team abandoned Jordan Field following the 1925 season, moving to Memorial Stadium for the 1926 outdoor track season. The baseball team soldiered on, but it was clear that Jordan Field wasn't exactly respected as hallowed ground. Then again, it hadn't held that status for a while.

For instance, during the 1922–23 school year, the IU marching band needed to raise money to take a trip to West Lafayette. The 1923 *Arbutus* pointed out that "it's pretty hard to get money out of students unless you have a novelty to offer them in return." So, naturally, the band turned to the most obvious way to draw a crowd and raise some money.

They held an auto polo event. You know, like regular polo, but using cars instead of horses. Seriously.

According to the November 18, 1922, *Indiana Daily Student*, two teams faced off in an auto polo match. Barrett Woodsmall and Joe Breeze hopped into a car they called Apollo Jr. to take on Methuselah, the car driven by Bill Pierce and a student by the name of Ernie Pyle—yep, *that* Ernie Pyle. The score was tied at one when Methuselah was forced to pull out of the match with engine troubles, thus ending the days of auto polo at Jordan Field.

Over the next couple of years, horse races were run at the field, and regular polo matches were held. When the 1925 silent film *Ben Hur* was released, IU students responded by holding chariot races at Jordan Field for entertainment.

Remnants of Jordan Field's life as a football stadium remained for years. The stumps of a goal post still stood in left field in 1928, and the field would occasionally be used by intramural teams. Baseball played second fiddle to the football and basketball programs on campus, and the team was forced to make do with what it had at Jordan Field through the 1930s. Baseball just wasn't much of a priority, and improvements were minimal. The Indiana Memorial Union sprang up close to the field in 1932, a fact that would prove ominous in the future.

Jordan Field enjoyed one last moment in the spotlight during World War II. With travel restrictions in place due to the war, the Cincinnati Reds and the Indianapolis Indians both held spring training in Bloomington from 1943 to 1945.

By the late 1940s, the university was looking to expand its athletic facilities. There already had been some talk about possibly moving all the facilities to an area north of the campus, and it seemed that was where the future lay when IU began building the baseball diamond that would later become Sembower Field on Fee Lane. The Crimson finally played their final game at Jordan Field during the 1950 season, ending the facility's days as a varsity sports complex.

Jordan Field still lived on for another decade as an intramural field. Lights were installed in the later years of its existence, but inevitably the march of progress was banging on the fences of the ancient complex.

The Biddle Continuation Center addition to the Indiana Memorial Union was in full swing by the late 1950s, and the university decided it would be best to provide Jordan Field with the cruelest death of all for an athletic facility—that of being made into a parking lot. During the summer of 1959, Jordan Field was paved over, and a huge piece of IU athletic history disappeared behind the gate of a toll booth. The lot still follows the contours of the field for the most part, and the grading that created the bowl shape of the field still exists to this day.

On October 11, 1980, Jordan Field received its gravestone. A marker was placed on the edge of the parking lot by the "I" Men's Association, and a dedication was read by IU president John W. Ryan during homecoming weekend. The marker still sits where it was placed, but the plaque has weathered, and the marker is slowly being covered by a large bush.

FIGURE 2.1. IU's first football team was established in 1886 by Arthur Woodford, a former player at Yale who was surprised that a team hadn't already been organized at Indiana. *IU Archives P0025595*

FIGURE 2.2. The 1894 football team featured halfback Preston Eagleson (top row, far left), who would be IU's first African American player on an officially sanctioned school team. *IU Archives P0056919*

FIGURE 2.3. Preston Eagleson was the second African American to graduate from IU, the first African American to graduate with an advanced degree, and IU's only African American athlete until 1931. *IU Archives P0022468*

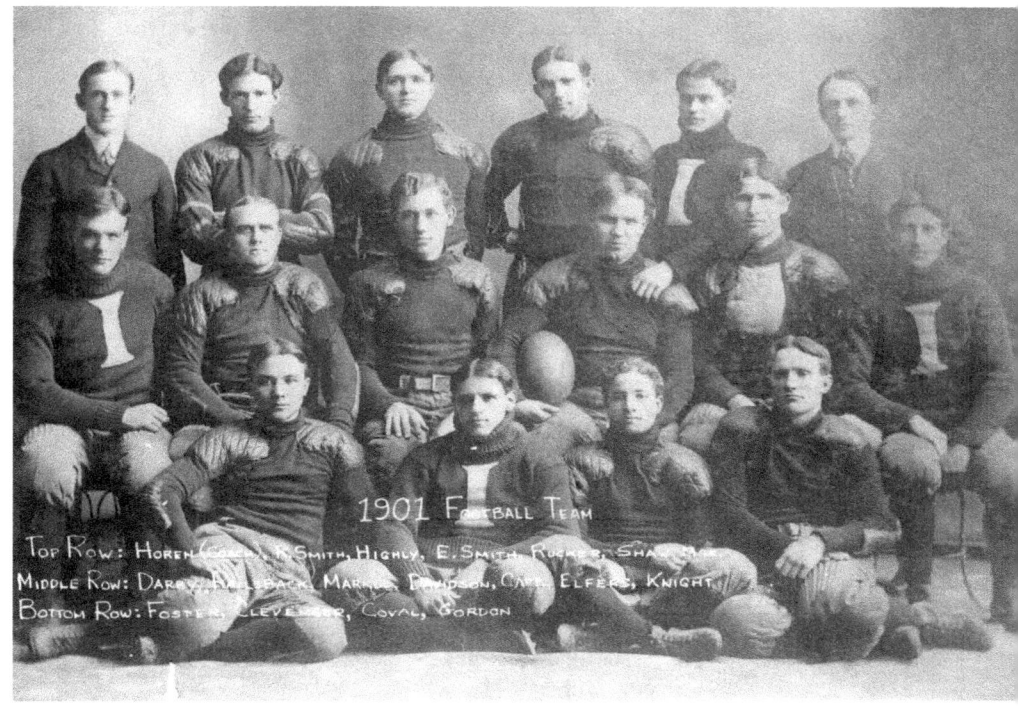

FACING TOP, FIGURE 2.4. Jordan Field was relatively crude by today's standards, but it would be the home for IU football for the first twenty-five years of the twentieth century. *IU Archives P0030984*

FACING BOTTOM, FIGURE 2.5. This drawing of Jordan Field appeared in the 1903 *Arbutus* yearbook and showcases the covered grandstands and simple bleachers. *IU Archives P0022793*

ABOVE, FIGURE 2.6. The 1901 football team set a scoring record that stands to this day by putting seventy-six points on Franklin College. *IU Archives P0025598*

FIGURE 2.7. Jordan Field was famous for its drainage issues, but that didn't stop IU from purposely flooding the field in the winter to provide a skating rink for students. *IU Archives P0056314*

3

The Birth of IU Basketball

The iconic candy-stripe pants. The five national championship banners. The packed Simon Skjodt Assembly Hall quaking as the thunderous noise of more than seventeen thousand fans rains down on opponents in a cacophony that makes it nearly impossible to hear yourself think, let alone communicate with a guy who is thirty feet away.

Every game day, every time an IU fan pulls on a cream-and-crimson jersey, grabs him- or herself a drink, and hunkers down to watch a game—and maybe yell at an official—that fan is carrying on a legacy that began in a dusty carpenter's shop behind Owen Hall on the Old Crescent part of Indiana's campus during the late nineteenth century when basketball was a new sport, and nobody really knew how to play.

But we'll get to that story in a minute. Before IU basketball could be born, the university needed to make a more serious investment in student recreation. It needed a place on the growing campus for students to gather—maybe they assembled—for various events, such as speeches, celebrations, and shows.

Maybe someplace like a new gymnasium.

When IU opened the Men's Gymnasium behind Owen Hall, it was a huge hit with students. However, it quickly became apparent that the gymnasium wasn't really big enough to accommodate the growing student population.

That population, by the way, was exploding. Student enrollment had doubled between 1888 and 1892, and it showed few signs of slowing down. Finding buildings that were big enough to hold all the students for major events was becoming a problem, and IU knew something had to be done.

In its biennial report filed in December 1892, IU reported that there simply needed to be more room for all the students. The report complained that Library Hall—which had been built in 1891 and would later be renamed Maxwell Hall—was already being forced into use as classroom space. Furthermore, the report stated that there was no assembly room where the students could meet in a body, and it was hoped that expansion of some of the facilities on campus could rectify that situation.

Despite the need, it would still take time for IU to take action to solve the problem. In fact, it took nearly four years for the administration to make a decision about what to do about the lack of space. In the meantime, Joseph Swain was named IU's ninth president in 1893, Kirkwood Hall was built in 1894, and the *Arbutus* was established.

Finally, in the summer of 1896, the administration turned to the dual problem of a lack of room for the student body to assemble and a lack of quality gymnasium space. It was clear that the original gymnasium, built just four years earlier, was woefully undersized for the growing student body, but that space could easily be converted for any other use, maybe even as a carpenter's shop. A new Men's Gymnasium would be built, with the building also serving as a meeting point for the student body.

On Monday, August 10, 1896, a contract was awarded to architect Philip Jeckel of Anderson, and Anderson contractor William E. Thompson was tapped to do the actual construction work. The general contract was for $10,310, and other items, including architect's fees, plumbing, wiring, and heating, amounted to another $1,700, bringing the total cost of the construction to $12,010. It was a major outlay of money, especially when you consider that the original Men's Gymnasium had been built four years earlier for a total of $1,000. (That $12,000 in 1896, by the way, translates to more than $365,000 in modern dollars.)

One day later, sharing the same page as reports that Sheriff Adams had thrashed his wheat the previous Friday and yielded eighteen bushels from twelve acres and that the same Sheriff Adams was housing just three prisoners in the county jail, the *Bloomington Telephone* broke the news of the new construction to the public. "After thoroughly considering the matter the Indiana University board of trustees have decided to erect a gymnasium hall," the August 11, 1896, *Bloomington Telephone* reported. "The immediate demand for the new building is that it may be used for a temporary chapel, and it is for this reason that it has finally been decided to commence work at once. . . . It is expected to commence excavation Monday morning. The new building is to be erected on a knoll southeast of Kirkwood Hall and will be one story, of frame, with a basement and substantial in every respect."

The paper went on to report that the building was to be outfitted with comfortable chairs that could seat twelve hundred people, and the expectation was that work would be finished October 1. "All lectures and public meetings will thereafter be held in this hall instead of the old college chapel," the *Telephone* finished.

Work began shortly thereafter on a building that was to be 125 feet long and 65 feet wide with a shingle roof. The main floor would be 90 feet long, and the building would include galleries along the north, south, and west ends. Posts held up the galleries on the three sides of the building. A stage was built at the east end of the building to allow convocations, theatrical productions, and other events to be held in the building. A dressing room was included, although it featured a dirt floor.

Unlike modern-day construction, the work on the new Men's Gymnasium proceeded rapidly. When the school term opened September 22, that day's *Telephone* reported that the incoming students, expected to near one thousand for the first time, could expect a wondrous new facility in the near future.

"The most important material improvement of the new campus made within the year is a beautiful new building, designed as a men's gymnasium," the *Telephone* said. "It was begun during the summer, and the returning students will see it on its way toward completion. For the present the main floor will be used as an assembly hall, accommodating two thousand people. The other rooms will be used at once for a gymnasium, and will be equipped with complete apparatus, shower baths and lockers."

As the students went through the fall semester, the building slowly rose out of the ground. In fact, construction was a little slower than expected. The October 1 completion date came and went without the building being finished. Mundane student life ran its course with the sound of hammering and sawing serving as the background.

The rival *Bloomington World* ran an illustration of what the gymnasium would look like as a finished product, and the paper reported that the new completion date would be November 1. It doesn't seem, however, that construction was finished by that day, either.

The December 8 edition of the *Telephone* carried the following announcement:

"The new gymnasium building to be used temporarily for a chapel will be dedicated the 18th by an entertainment under the management of the Glee club. The lower floor is to be gaily decorated and the occasion is to be made one of the most interesting of the college year."

The proceeds from the dedication would be split, with 60 percent going to the Glee Club, 20 percent to the Athletic Association, and the other 20 percent going to the contest committee.

Just four days after Governor-Elect James A. Mount came out emphatically against continuing to allow football to be played in the state of Indiana, the new Men's Gymnasium was unveiled to the public.

"THE EVENT OF THE SEASON," screamed a headline in the December 19 edition of the *World*.

"The new University building was dedicated last evening in the presence of the largest audience that ever assembled under one roof in Bloomington," the *World* reported. "The immense room was appropriately decorated with cream and crimson—the colors of the University. The mammoth flag of Wicks & Co. hung gracefully at the back of the stage, and the championship football flag of 1896 occupied a prominent space."

The hall was decorated with streamers of cream and crimson, and palms and other floral decorations filled every nook and open space in the building. The space was also lit by 150 electric lights, which "made the room almost as light as day," according to the *World*. Fraternities reserved sections of seating and arrived as single bodies.

Then, at 8:15 p.m., the Glee Club made its entrance to a loud ovation, and President Swain received the same when he entered a few moments later. Swain moved to the front of the stage, and without any notes, he addressed the crowd. He said:

> We have met tonight for a double purpose. First, to give a hearty greeting to the Glee Club of Indiana University. I need not sing its praises. It will speak for itself in tones that are louder, in notes that are sweeter and with accents more pleasing than any words of mine. May its voices be heard throughout the length and breadth of the commonwealth.
>
> In the second place, we have met to dedicate this new gymnasium. The erection of this building solved, for the present, three important questions: First, Mitchell Hall can now be used for the Women's Gymnasium. Second, ample room will be provided for a Men's Gymnasium for several years to come. Third, with some inconvenience an ample audience room for large assemblies is provided until the demands of the work in physical training require the whole building. With the present outlook this whole building will soon be needed for the legitimate work of physical training. No better demonstration of the vitality of this work could be given than the fact that the Women's Gymnasium has prospered in a cellar and the Men's Gymnasium in a barn.

Swain stressed the importance of physical fitness in the training of a college student, and he thanked Thompson and Jeckel for their hard work on the project. He closed by making a not-so-subtle hint that the new building, while nice, didn't necessarily meet all of his expectations or solve all of IU's problems.

"I wish to thank the people of Indiana that they have had the wisdom to provide this building for the use of their children," Swain said. "If we are faithful to their highest welfare, I am sure that the people, in turn, will care for our needs and one day give us a permanent assembly room worthy of the University and the State."

The program proceeded with a musical program that included performances by the Glee Club, a violin solo, and a song about the "amusing travesty on the feline tribe."

The night closed with a Glee Club rendition of "Silent Night, Holy Night," which prompted the *World* to rave that "clearly no programme [sic] ever given in this city has been more favorably received." Unfortunately, the glow surrounding the new Men's Gymnasium wouldn't last all that long.

The new Men's Gym served its purpose well during the few years following its opening, but as enrollment continued to grow, so did the number of athletic teams. That meant that space in the gym was becoming limited, and juggling all the sports made scheduling difficult. Not only were regular gym classes being held, but baseball needed an indoor facility in which to practice and stay in shape, and the track team needed to get out of the cold in the winter to prepare for the upcoming season.

The founding of the new basketball team created an even bigger crunch when it came to space. As the team prepared for its first season, the *Indiana University Student* newspaper noted that push was starting to come to shove from a space standpoint in the Men's Gymnasium. "The work Saturday morning consisted of baseball, basket ball and track work," the January 28, 1901, edition reported. "Each day brings out the fact that we do not have near enough room for the various athletic teams. The basket ball men have learned the game and are now working on the finer points of the game in order to be able to take advantage of every possible play."

Shuffling between the different sports took some coordination. After all, with the track team actually running hurdles in the gymnasium and baseball knocking balls around, the gym could be a dangerous place.

Besides being home to the basketball program, the Men's Gymnasium hosted hundreds of events through the years. On January 18, 1904, William Butler Yeats, one of the foremost literary figures of the twentieth century, performed at the Gymnasium, and IU president William Lowe Bryan, who succeeded Swain, was inaugurated at the Men's Gymnasium in 1903. As time went on, there was a movement to try to find a better name for the facility than simply the Men's Gymnasium. A note from the IU Archives from March 27, 1900, that is listed only as being from "President Rep. to Bal," suggests renaming the building: "It would be more convenient to have a name for the Men's Gymnasium. I would suggest for the consideration of the Trustees the propriety of calling this building Foster Hall in honor of the Hon. John W. Foster, one of our honored alumni who takes a great interest in the University. He has showed his renewed interest this year by giving $50 for the Foster prize and allowing this year's interest to be added to the fund."

The suggestion, however, was ignored. Naming something on the IU campus after Foster wasn't. In 1963, the newest dormitory on campus was named the John W. Foster Quadrangle in his honor.

Despite the fact the basketball team improved as the years went on, crowds were small due to a lack of space. The galleries could hold four hundred people, and although an additional twelve hundred could pack the main floor, comfort was difficult to come by. Playing basketball in the Men's Gymnasium also was a bit challenging and more than a little dangerous. Because it wasn't designed with basketball in mind, the posts that held up the galleries created dangerous obstacles just a few feet from the sideline. Saving a ball was fraught with trouble, and fans had to deal with obstructed views if they watched from the main floor. Floor burns, by the way, didn't exist back then. There wasn't a true finish on the floor, and the floorboards were badly scuffed, leading to more than a few skinned knees and splinters when players went to the ground for the ball. Records also show that a swimming pool was installed in the building in 1909, although the pool didn't last long. A stage was later constructed to cover the pool, but we'll get to that in a minute.

The students, meanwhile, were starting to sour on the Men's Gymnasium after only fifteen years. The 1911 *Arbutus* credits a professor for doing the best he can in a less-than-perfect situation. "Through the efforts of Dr. (C.P.) Hutchins (the head of physical training), the gymnasium, which we hope is nearing the close of its existence, has been improved in many ways. The addition of new apparatus and lockers, the building of the new pool and showers, as well as the strict discipline enforced have done much toward the formation of an ideal system of athletics and physical training."

The limitations of space continued to be frustrating for students, but a major change was in the works for the building.

By 1914, the building was in its eighteenth year of operation and was starting to show its age. In an effort to update and improve the cultural impact of the facility, construction began on a modern addition to the Men's Gymnasium. The pool, which had been popular for five years, was covered during the fall when a new stage measuring sixty-five feet long and twenty-six feet deep was built at a cost of $3,500.

The IU *Alumni Quarterly* from January 1915 reported on the renovation by saying a "fully-equipped stage and auditorium has been for many years one of the most crying needs of the University."

"During the latter part of November and the first week of December, a large squad of carpenters was busy tearing out partitions, extending the north and south walls, and raising the roof of the east end of the Men's Gymnasium," the *Quarterly* reported. "Now a new stagehouse towers high above the old building, the peak of the roof being nearly sixty feet above the floor level."

The latest in fire protection, including an asbestos fire curtain that could be lowered at a moment's notice and a curtain of water that could be sprayed on the stage, were added for safety. The building was rewired with iron conduits—previously wires weren't sheathed in anything in the walls of the building—and the exits were doubled.

The *Quarterly* praised the renovation but noted that "permanent relief will come only with the building of a complete modern auditorium, but no small degree of temporary relief is afforded by the increased room and advantage of the rebuilt gymnasium."

The *Quarterly* couldn't have imagined that it would be more than twenty years before a new auditorium would be built on campus.

Still, in the short term, the work paid off, with Maude Adams—by far the most popular stage actress of the day—christening the new stage with a performance of *The Legend of Leonora* on December 7, 1914. The performance was hailed as a major milestone in improving the culture in Bloomington and would lead to other major acts passing through town in the coming years.

The addition of the stage, however, signaled that the era of sports in the Men's Gymnasium was quickly drawing to an end. Students, in fact, were already plotting to convince the administration that a new gymnasium was needed. In the spring of 1915, the students tried to use a clever ruse to get what they wanted, even if they had to lean on the military to do it, as reported by the *Alumni Quarterly* from April of that year:

> A much discussed project during the term just closed was one to establish at the University a battalion of the Indiana National Guard, to be known as the Indiana University battalion. Some four hundred students of the University put their names to a paper stating their willingness to join the proposed organization, and the approval of the faculty was asked for this use of the grounds and the University name.
>
> After considerable discussion and investigation by a committee to which the proposal was referred, the faculty on March 13 by a substantial majority voted its disapproval of the project. This decision was based in the main upon the view that it was inexpedient for the University by formal action to encourage young men while still engaged in their college studies to take upon themselves the obligations of a three-years enlistment in the State militia. There was also a feeling that a very considerable part of the students who signed the paper were not so much interested in the formation of a university military organization as they were in securing for the University an Armory which could be used as a men's gymnasium—a result which, it was urged, would follow the organization of the University battalion.

The plot, though denied, still managed to find a happy ending. One day before the faculty was called upon to vote, the board of trustees authorized the erection of a new gymnasium for male students as soon as funds were available. Indiana would get its modern gym after all.

The Crimson played their last home basketball game at the Men's Gymnasium January 5, 1917, hammering Rose Poly 35–9. The opening of the new Men's Gymnasium—we know it's confusing, but blame IU, not us—brought about the end of sports at the old gym, but its days of usefulness were far from over.

In an effort to end the confusion over the old Men's Gymnasium and new Men's Gymnasium, it was sometime during this period that the former Men's Gymnasium was renamed Assembly Hall. It continued to host theatrical events, commencement ceremonies, and other events, but the arrival of the Great War (later to be known as World War I) pressed Assembly Hall into much more important action.

First, the Spanish Flu pandemic swept over the world, and the disease actually shut down IU for a month in late 1918. During that time, the Student Army Training Corps used Assembly Hall as a hospital, with rows and rows of beds being placed on the main floor and in the galleries to handle the sick and dying. "Skilled medical attention was given to the men when they became ill," the 1919 *Arbutus* wrote. "The women of Bloomington performed faithful service at the University Hospital in Assembly Hall, taking great interest in rendering any service which was in their power to the sick men at that place."

Beds were often placed outside of the building to allow them to air out after sick men had lain in them, and all efforts were made to keep the students healthy.

As the years progressed, Assembly Hall's star began to fade as it aged. For some reason, the building became the repeated target of threats of arson. Deans of Men C. E. Edmondson and C. J. Sembower received an envelope December 4, 1930, on which was written, "Dear President—It would be no surprise if students burn Assembly Hall when they are incited by such stuff as this." Enclosed in the envelope was a newspaper article detailing the fact that IU had beaten Purdue 7–6 in the Old Oaken Bucket game, and Albert Stump, a two-time Democratic candidate for senator, had used the victory to claim that it was proof that things were going to be different now that Democratic president Franklin Roosevelt would be taking over. The article went on to quote Uz McMurtrie and Wayne Stackhouse, two local residents who were in attendance for Stump's comments.

Stackhouse described both the celebration following the Bucket win and the precautions that were taken against the burning of Assembly Hall, which was said to be "an ancient frame structure which is the university's only auditorium." McMurtrie seemed to favor arson.

"That is what we have needed down there for a long time," McMurtrie said in the clipping. "I only wished they had burned down that old building. It would have been a sure sign that the revolution had set in."

Assembly Hall was never set on fire, but it couldn't escape the march of progress. On March 21, 1938, the board of trustees ordered that the building be demolished to make way for a parking lot outside of the six-year-old Memorial Union. The March 22, 1938, *Telephone* lamented its passing by bringing up its history as the site of the first state high school basketball tournament, but it also called the facility a "ramshackle campus landmark."

Once the building was actually being demolished, the sentiment was a little stronger for one of the most important campus buildings of the first half of the twentieth century. A poem appeared in the *Indianapolis Star* remembering the building, and the 1938 *IU Winter Alumni Quarterly* lamented its passing under the headline "That Old Barn":

> Assembly Hall is going down, board by board. No longer need officials worry for fear football enthusiasts will burn it down; no longer will visitors to the campus wonder about the why and wherefore of such a structure boasting of many handsome buildings.
>
> But shed a tear for Assembly Hall. Once the Men's Gymnasium, it was here that the state basketball tournament was born and nourished until it outgrew these quarters. Here hundreds of graduates received their diplomas, sometimes to the strains of "Then You'll Remember Me." Here many of the most famous actors, musicians and orators have appeared on its stage, which was made over in 1914 to enable Maude Adams to give a performance. And now the ether which once carried the cultivated voices of a Drew, a Sandburg, a Beveridge, a Breslau will be filled with motor honks and exhausts and other noises heard in all parking spaces. Sic transit Gloria mundi.

"Sic transit Gloria mundi," by the way, is a Latin phrase meaning "Thus passes the glory of the world."

The original Assembly Hall was the birthplace of IU basketball, but how did the storied program come about? As was the case in those early years, IU's habit of being an early adopter when it came to sports is at the forefront.

The baseball team was founded right as the sport gained in popularity following the Civil War. The same is true for the establishment of the football team as chronicled in chapter 2. The roots of IU basketball begin just ten years after James Naismith created the game. Unlike baseball and football, which evolved organically into the games we know today, basketball was born as a fresh activity with mostly the same structure in place. There are no legends surrounding the invention of basketball. There is a clear history.

James Naismith was a thirty-one-year-old second-year graduate student at the International YMCA Training School (now known as Springfield College) in Springfield, Massachusetts, in the winter of 1891. He was studying the new field of physical education under Dr. Luther Halsey Gulick, who was superintendent of physical education at the college, and Naismith answered Gulick's call to develop a new indoor game "that would be interesting, easy to learn, and easy to play in the winter and by artificial light."

Naismith asked a janitor if he could find a couple of eighteen-inch-square boxes to use as goals, and his students could throw a ball into the boxes to score points. The janitor didn't have any boxes, but he did have a couple of peach baskets. Naismith took those peach baskets, nailed them to the balcony—which happened to be ten feet high—on either end of the gymnasium, and drew up thirteen rules for the game. His secretary typed up the rules and pinned them to the bulletin board.

"Basket ball," as it was then known, was born.

The game quickly gained popularity thanks to the system of YMCAs across the country, and less than ten years later, it would already be on IU's campus.

The game was already being played on a recreational basis in the women's gymnasium when a student named Thomas Records entered IU in the fall of 1899. Records had spent time as a squad leader at the Terre Haute, Indiana, YMCA, and he introduced himself to Director of Athletics James Horne. Horne was the coach of all sports at IU, and when the end of the football season rolled around, Records called a meeting for students who were interested in playing basketball as a varsity sport.

"The Men's Gym was used for all assemblies and so was not available for the first meeting," Records reported more than fifty years later in an article published in the April 1958 *Indiana Alumni Magazine*. "We got together in a carpenter shop which had been used as a gym before the Men's Gym had been built."

The gathering, however, wasn't exactly held in the best of circumstances, and it's not like everyone was gathered around a table to talk about putting together a team. Instead, the eighty to ninety prospective players—an impressive number, considering fewer than seven hundred students were enrolled at IU at the time—showed up at the carpenter's shop, and an explanation of the rules was made. Then the students were divided into groups and were given a ball. The carpenters who were working in the shop at the time took full advantage of the situation.

"The carpenters were working there though it was Saturday afternoon, but finding they were having to dodge the ball too much, they knocked off," Records wrote. "I kept the whistle blowing to stop near-fights, etc., or to explain the rules. Finally, I had to call off practice at five o'clock."

Unfortunately, but not surprisingly, basketball wasn't a priority for the university at the time. Records wrote that finding equipment or a place to play wasn't easy, and even when the team did find a time and place to practice, it came with its own set of challenges.

"The Men's Gym (the original Assembly Hall) was seated with benches with iron legs, and these had to be taken off for practice and replaced afterwards," Records wrote. "Then the president of the University would not permit us to put goals up or even to paint the lines on the floor."

Like good Hoosiers, they adapted and adjusted. Goals were placed on large, heavy platforms that could be moved around, solving the problem of not being allowed to hang a hoop. Next, instead of painting lines, chalk lines were placed on the floor as a temporary measure.

"Even with this extra work, we had plenty of material," Records wrote. "I soon began selecting a first team."

Everything seemed to be going according to plan, but there was one thing neither Records nor Horne could have anticipated.

"Before we scheduled any games, small pox broke out, and everyone had to be vaccinated," Records wrote. "Most of the boys on the team developed sore arms, which ended the season of 1899–1900."

IU's basketball program was down, but it wasn't out.

The next fall, Records was back to leading gym classes, but in the middle of the football season, he felt he needed to help the team. Records stepped into the lineup at center against Purdue for the last game of the season, and he helped IU score a win in that Thanksgiving Day game.

Victory in hand, Records turned to organizing what would become IU's marquee program.

In January 1901, Records and Horne held the very first official basketball practice, and by early February, the team was tuning up to start the season.

"The old gymnasium is now cleaned out, and the basketball men commence work in it Tuesday afternoon for the first time," wrote the February 7, 1901, *Indiana Daily Student*. "Practice Tuesday and this afternoon was very brisk with few fouls. A game was played yesterday morning at 11:00. It will be the last hard work before the team leaves for Indianapolis. They will leave Friday morning and play at the YMCA gymnasium."

Indiana's first-ever opponent would be Butler.

"Much interest is manifested in tomorrow's basketball contest at Indianapolis," the *Indiana Daily Student* wrote. "It will be the first game that our team has played this year, and the outcome, while reasonably certain, is nevertheless a matter of conjecture. Our team will no doubt win a victory, but just how far superior to the other teams remains to be demonstrated."

The *Indiana Daily Student* was confident. Records, not so much.

"Often in practice we just did not take the trouble to drag those heavy platforms out, so we passed most of the time," Records wrote in the April 1958 *Indiana Alumni Magazine*. "In every game, Indiana would rush to the front without losing (the ball) only to miss many attempts at the goal."

The first IU basketball team was made up of Phelps Darby, Ernest Strange, Jay Fitzgerald, Alvah J. Rucker, Charles Unnewehr, and Earl Walker. Horne was the team's coach, and Records served as the squad's manager, although he does appear in IU's official records as having played in 1901. The players bought their own equipment, and they weren't awarded letters because the faculty didn't consider basketball to be a collegiate sport.

The game back then, by the way, was very, very different than we know it now. Beside the fact a jump ball was held after every basket, few teams spent much time dribbling the ball, and there wasn't a ten-second rule to cross the midline of the court, mainly because there was no midline. Also, when a ball went out of bounds, it wasn't turned over by the team that last touched it. Instead, it belonged to the player who got to it first.

"This made it necessary for every man in the vicinity to rush after the ball, which was pretty rough stuff," Records wrote.

The glorious history of Indiana basketball opened with a 22–17 loss to Butler, but the defeat didn't dampen the enthusiasm on campus.

"Our first game of basket ball was played at the Indianapolis YMCA gymnasium Friday afternoon in the presence of a good crowd of college students drawn to the city by the State Oratorical Contest," the February 11, 1901, *Indiana Daily Student* wrote. "It was Indiana's first game, and the team lost mainly through inaccuracy throwing for goals. In teamwork, Indiana played a better and cleaner game, and not until the last three minutes of the last half was the final result at all certain."

The *Indiana Daily Student* reported that "the Butlerites, by a trick pass, succeeded in throwing three goals in less than that many minutes, making the final score 22–17."

IU's official records, by the way, show IU losing 20–17. It's up to you which source you believe, but the contemporary student newspaper account says 22–17.

In fact, Indiana lost its first three games—a February 28 rematch vs. Butler in IU's first home game, and it lost 20–15 at Purdue on March 1. The first victory for the program came March 8 in Bloomington in a 26–17 win over Wabash. By the way, things got chippy in that Purdue game.

"Two opposing players took a swing at each other," Records wrote. "That always called for an expulsion, but the referee blew his whistle and stood bouncing the ball and looking at the two men. They stuck out their hands and shook hands and the game went on. The referee was a good sport."

What happened following the win over Wabash is up for debate. IU's official records show Indiana losing a March 15 game at Purdue 23–19, and Purdue's official records lists a 23–19 win over IU at Purdue on March 15.

So what's the problem?

Well, Records wrote in the 1950s, "The last game, we beat Wabash by ten points." More importantly is the report of the season from the 1901 *Arbutus*. "The games scheduled with Wabash and Purdue, later in the same month, were declared off, and the season ended at Indiana," the *Arbutus* wrote.

There is also no contemporary account of the game in the *Indiana Daily Student*, the Bloomington papers, or the Lafayette or Indianapolis papers.

So, what happened? It's difficult to say without source material. IU and Purdue's records both say the game happened, but records from that time are notoriously inaccurate (see the conflicting record of the final score of the first game). Once a mistake is made, that mistake tends to be copied over time, and when enough time passes, such an error is set in stone.

The one contemporary account of the season from the *Arbutus*, supported by the comment from Records himself, suggests the March 15 game at Purdue—which would have been the second game AT Purdue that year, a fact that seems extremely unlikely since every other opponent was a home-and-away situation—never happened.

The official records say the program went 1–4 overall in 1901. History says that record is 1–3.

IU did suffer an early tragedy in its program.

Ernest Strange came to IU in 1899 from Anderson, Indiana. He was the son of Joshua Strange, who was one of Grant County's most prominent farmers and one of the wealthiest men in the area. Ernest's uncle, John, was an attorney in Marion, Indiana, and his brother, Leonard, was a dentist.

In other words, the future looked bright for Ernest, who took an interest in the new game of basketball. He went out for the 1901 team, and he was good enough to be named captain. He scored nine points in the first-ever IU basketball game—that's more than half of Indiana's total of seventeen points—and he played a crucial role in IU's first-ever basketball victory.

Strange was the team's leading scorer, and there were high hopes about what he could accomplish during his junior year.

Only he never returned to Bloomington.

A few days after going home for the summer to work on his family's farm, Ernest was helping with some chores when a boiler operating a feed grinder exploded. A piece of metal rocketed toward Ernest, striking him in the head. Just a few minutes later, the promising life of Ernest Strange was over.

He was twenty-one.

The basketball team continued, with Phelps Darby taking over as head coach, and IU went on to post a 4–4 record in its second season. A year later, in 1903, IU went 8–4 overall to push the program above .500 for the first time, and it did so on the back of Indiana's first real basketball star, a lanky freshman center out of Indianapolis by the name of Leslie "Doc" Maxwell.

Maxwell was born May 19, 1884, to Dr. Allison Maxwell and the former Cynthia Routh. Allison Maxwell was born in Bloomington, graduated from IU with honors in 1868, and taught briefly at the school before leaving to find his fortune in California and Ohio and then returning to Indianapolis. Like his family before him, he found it in medicine, and he eventually helped found the Indiana University School of Medicine, where he served as its first dean. His family's association with medicine went back generations, earning Leslie the "Doc" nickname.

(Fun fact: Maxwell's lineage is fascinating. His family was filled with doctors—uncles, cousins, etc., hence the nickname—and his great-great-grandfather, Bezaleel, was a Revolutionary War soldier who was present at the surrender of Yorktown. Bezaleel had a son, David, who grew up to be a doctor and married a woman named Mary Dunn. In 1818, David Maxwell bought a lot in Bloomington, and he moved to the city the next year. They eventually built the first brick house in Bloomington along what is now College Avenue. Mary's family moved to Bloomington in 1823, establishing a large farm on land that is the current home of the campus of IU. Dunn Meadow? Yes, that's them. David served on IU's board of trustees for thirty years; he was president of the board for twenty-eight years, and Maxwell Hall is named after him. The oldest of his eleven children, James, was a doctor, and he was Allison's father.)

Considering his family's long relationship with IU, it's not surprising Leslie Maxwell would end up at Indiana. How Maxwell ended up on the basketball team, however, is unknown. Records from this era are extremely sketchy due to a fire that consumed nearly all the contemporary copies of the *Indiana Daily Student*, but there's no dispute that he made an immediate impact on the team.

The Crimson opened the 1903 season with a 28–16 win over Butler on January 14, and they followed that with road losses to Wabash and Crawfordsville Business College. Their next outing would be a special event.

Basketball had already captured the hearts and minds of people in Indiana, and IU was ready to elevate the sport as a way to draw people to Bloomington. That's why, as part of the January 20, 1903, Founder's Day celebration, a basketball game with DePauw was scheduled for 9:30 a.m. to serve as an appetizer for the afternoon's main festivities—the inauguration of William Lowe Bryan as IU's tenth university president.

The Tuesday dawned with a threat of showers or even some snow, but that didn't stop hundreds of people from crowding the Men's Gymnasium to see the game. Maxwell, playing just his fourth career game for IU, put on a show that would be remembered for years.

"DePauw Given a Drubbing," read the headline of the January 23, 1903, *Indiana Daily Student*. "The Methodists Do Not Have a Chance with Indiana at Basket Ball."

The story continued.

"Basket ball has taken such a prominent place in athletics at Indiana of late that it was thought advisable to schedule a game to be played during the Foundation Day exercises. Accordingly, a game was arranged to be played at nine o'clock Tuesday morning. The game was well attended by visitors and was a fair representation of Indiana athletics."

IU dominated DePauw, setting a school single-game scoring record in a 43–9 victory. More importantly for our story, Maxwell dominated the action for IU. He scored thirteen field goals, and he added a free throw to finish with twenty-seven points.

"Maxwell for the Varsity played by far the best game, at least, if throwing goals is a criterion," the *Indiana Daily Student* wrote.

No record was kept of how Maxwell scored, whether it be on lay-ups, outside shots, or in the paint. There also is no record of how many shots he took to make his thirteen field goals. But despite the lack of coverage on the specifics, there was a general feeling of optimism about the team.

"The Varsity put up a good game of ball, but it could be seen that they did not play their limit," the *Indiana Daily Student* wrote. "The team work of Indiana is improving steadily and prospects for a good team grow more flattering with each day's practice."

Maxwell had tripled the opposing team's point total, and he would go on to be a key to IU's success that season. He was, however, held scoreless against on Purdue January 30 while giving up thirty-five points to the Boilers' J. Miller in a 51–16 loss.

Maxwell would be named captain for the 1904 season, but he missed the 1905 campaign after suffering an injury during football season that kept him out of action for basketball. He returned for the 1906 season and, along with Godfred Ritterskamp and Chester Harmeson, made up part of what was considered the best frontcourt in the state.

The senior saw his scoring record actually broken by Harmeson on January 27, 1906, when Harmeson dropped in twenty-eight points in a 46–21 win over the New Albany YMCA. However, as the YMCA isn't a collegiate entity, Maxwell remained IU's official record holder.

It wasn't a record he would give up easily.

Maxwell remained IU's single-game scoring leader for thirty-five years, holding the mark until Ernie Andres scored thirty points in a win over Illinois on March 4, 1938, to break the Big Ten single-game scoring record and win a league scoring title in the process.

Maxwell's athletic achievements came to an end when he graduated in 1906, but he went on to a long and fruitful life as a doctor. He served as a captain in the US Army during World War I, and he founded the first hospital in Broward County, Florida. Maxwell passed away in June 1950 at the age of sixty-six.

As the game of basketball changed and scoring increased, Maxwell's record output was quickly lost to the mists of time. But the fact remains that only one IU player, Jimmy Rayl, has held the school's single-game scoring record for longer than Maxwell. Rayl's fifty-six-point outing in 1962 set Indiana's current all-time mark, and he matched that total the next season as well. More than half a century has passed since Rayl first set the mark, but still in firm second place are the twenty-seven points Maxwell scored, a mark that lasted thirty-five years.

FIGURE 3.1. The opening of the new Men's Gymnasium—the future original Assembly Hall—raised the profile of IU athletics and gave the basketball team a permanent home. *IU Archives P0020440*

FIGURE 3.2. This photo from 1897 showcases the interior of the future Assembly Hall, when it was packed for an event. *IU Archives P0020439*

FIGURE 3.3. James Horne arrived as the director of athletics in the late 1800s and helped found the basketball program while also bringing IU athletics into the twentieth century. *IU Archives P0021178*

FIGURE 3.4. The 1901 IU basketball team, the first ever organized at the university. *IU Archives P0020320*

FIGURE 3.5. Leslie "Doc" Maxwell (center with the basketball), shown with the 1904 team, became IU's first scoring star who set a record that lasted decades. *IU Archives P0020323*

4

Tragedy and Triumph

By the early 1900s, football at Indiana was solidly established.

It was in a stable conference. The sport was a foundation of the university, and the student body and fans turned out in droves to see games. No, attendance wasn't what it would become, and college football was a shadow of the sport that we know, but it garnered headlines and drew attention every year.

It wasn't the safest sport, but that was some of the draw.

Nearly two dozen players pounded into one another for sixty solid minutes, and although there was some padding, and the players wore leather helmets (without face protection), it was a tough man's sport.

As is the case now, broken bones, torn ligaments, sprains, and bruises were common. Modern medicine makes most of those issues almost routine, and life-threatening situations rarely develop.

That wasn't always the case. In the early days of college football, life-threatening injuries were common, and even the smallest problem could turn into something major.

During the first decade of the twentieth century, college football found itself under assault by critics who said the game was too dangerous to be played by anyone. Player deaths were commonplace. Two college players died in both 1906 and 1907, six died in 1908, and ten were killed during the 1909 season.

Not all the deaths actually occurred on the field, and most came long after the game had ended. Indiana, unfortunately, lands on the list of schools affected by the death of a player during the 1909 season.

As training for the 1909 season opened, James Sheldon was excited.

Indiana's head coach took in the late September air at Jordan Field and was pleased with what he saw. It was September 21, 1909, and IU had never welcomed a bigger group of players to its first football practice of the season. A total of forty-four players came out for the team, and more than two hundred onlookers watched the Crimson go through their paces from the wooden bleachers along the sideline.

After going 3–4 overall and 1–3 in the Western Conference in 1908, optimism couldn't have been higher for Sheldon's squad. IU's offensive line was back intact save for one starter, and former captain Scott Paddock had been replaced with a freshman, Thomas Andrew "Andy" Gill, who seemed poised to make an immediate impact. Both of IU's ends, including Arthur "Cotton" Berndt, were back as well, and Sheldon was poised to use them.

In a nod to the changing winds of college football, Sheldon planned to make the forward pass a bigger part of his offense. It was a risky move. The forward pass had only been legalized three years earlier in an effort to open the game and make it safer, and it came with a number of rules. Passes could only be thrown to the outside of the field, and they had to be caught by a player more than five yards past the line of scrimmage, or it would be ruled a turnover. A throw that touched the ground without hitting anyone also resulted in a turnover, and a pass that touched an offensive player but fell incomplete resulted in a fifteen-yard penalty. Oh, and passes caught in the end zone were ruled a touchback.

Despite the risks, Sheldon decided throwing the ball could solve some of IU's offensive problems. Indiana scored just forty-three points during the 1908 season, and the Crimson suffered through a three-game stretch late in the year in which they were shut out by Wisconsin, Illinois, and Notre Dame. With only three downs to gain ten yards—on a field 110 yards in length from goal line-to-goal line, mind you—Sheldon needed to find a way to move the ball at least into field goal range without beating up his players (1909, by the way, was the first season in which field goals were worth three points. Previously, they had been worth four points. Touchdowns back then were worth five points, plus there was an extra point attempt).

Sheldon's team worked on the forward pass with right halfback Howard Paddock showing particular skill. He was ambidextrous, and his left-handed passes were described as "remarkable" by the *Daily Student.* The Crimson impressed Sheldon enough that he provided a bit of early bulletin-board material for one of IU's biggest rivals.

"We have the best chance we have ever hard to beat Chicago," Sheldon said.

In the early part of the twentieth century, few teams could match the power and pure innovation of Amos Alonzo Stagg's Chicago Maroons. The Maroons had won three of the previous four Western Conference titles and a national championship in 1905, and Sheldon, a former player for Stagg, knew full well Indiana had never beaten Chicago in seven previous tries. In fact, the Crimson had been outscored in those games 234–25, including a 29–6 whipping in 1908.

Still, Sheldon had a feeling about his team. The players were as crisp as ever following a long summer away from the gridiron.

One of those crisp players, however, wouldn't make it to the end of the first game. George Frank "Duke" Trimble was born April 22, 1883, in St. Lawrence, South Dakota. His parents moved the family to Evansville, Indiana, somewhere along the way, and after graduating from Evansville High School in 1901, Trimble spent a year teaching and helping his father, William, on the family farm. During the spring of 1903, he enrolled at IU, but he had to drop out in 1905 following his father's death. He returned to school in 1907, quickly picking up his busy social life. He was a member of the Glee Club, a forward on the basketball team for two years, and a guard for the football team.

He focused on physics in the classroom, but he loved football. Trimble was excited to be a part of a 1909 Crimson team that was expected to challenge for a Western Conference title, and he went into the team's scrimmage Saturday, September 25, ready to make his presence felt.

Seven days later, he was dead.

Trimble had scored some new football cleats for the new season, but they weren't quite broken in after three days of practice. During the scrimmage, the back of his shoe rubbed on the heel of one of his feet, giving him a blister. He missed practice Monday, and he wasn't feeling well. By Tuesday afternoon, his leg had swelled to twice its normal size, and that night he was admitted to the hospital.

Indianapolis Dr. E. D. Clark took a train to Bloomington to examine Trimble, and it was immediately clear to him that his patient was suffering from blood poisoning. Trimble was given a one-in-fifty chance of pulling through, but doctors did everything medical science in the early twentieth century could do. Thursday morning saw doctors make fifteen different incisions in Trimble's leg, cuts that totaled a length of roughly five feet, in an effort to drain the wound and keep the infection from spreading to the rest of Trimble's body.

At first there was some hope that Trimble might make it after all. The *Daily Student* reported that Trimble's fever had gradually lowered to around one hundred degrees, and "all indications point to improvement." The crowd attending "Yell" practice at Jordan Field was told Trimble was getting better, a fact that soothed a lot of worried people.

Except it wasn't true. Even as teammates and friends flooded the hospital, they weren't told the severity of Trimble's condition.

Friday saw Trimble continue to fight the illness, but he took a turn for the worse Friday night and early Saturday morning. Doctors believed he was near death early in the day, but oxygen kept Trimble alive.

As kickoff for IU's game against DePauw approached, Trimble became delirious and tried to get out to bed to play in the game. He had to be held down in bed by his mother and doctors, even as a priest was being summoned. Teammates stopped by to check on Trimble before the game, and their presence only upset Trimble more. They still were not told how serious his condition was.

Indiana's game against DePauw kicked off at 3:00 p.m. on October 2, and when the final gun sounded that afternoon, Indiana walked off a 28–5 winner.

The final gun on the life of Frank Trimble, however, went off at 4:08 p.m. that same afternoon. He was surrounded by his mother and his extended family.

The team wasn't told until after the game.

Trimble's death rocked the IU community. A service for him was held in Bloomington, and the church was overflowing. University officials were on hand, and the celebration of Trimble's life was a tear-filled event. He was buried in Evansville.

Trimble's story wouldn't have happened today. He would have received antibiotics and been closely monitored by team doctors, and he almost certainly wouldn't have met his end. But Trimble didn't enjoy the luxury of playing in the twenty-first century. Instead, a blister sent him to his doom, a fact that should be a reminder to everyone that we live in an age of medical wonder.

The tragedy of the death of Trimble overshadowed the first game of the 1909 season, but the Crimson looked good in that opener, needing just four minutes to score their first touchdown of the season. Gill, the talented freshman, went around left end for a ten-yard TD run, giving IU a 6–0 lead. DePauw quickly answered with a score of its own, but it missed the extra point, leaving IU up 6–5.

That lead grew to 17–5 by halftime, and Indiana continued to march after the break. IU scored twice more, sending the nearly three hundred DePauw supporters home on their special train in a sour mood.

The mighty, mighty Maroons were next on IU's schedule, and Sheldon felt like the season rode on that game. If the Crimson could just break through against Chicago, everything could change for the program.

Sheldon pushed his players harder than ever and even brought in arc lights to illuminate Jordan Field. Using a ball that had been painted white, Sheldon worked his team, according to the *Daily Student*, until "half-past supper time," mostly focusing on the offensive line.

When Saturday rolled around, the Crimson earned the praise of everyone who saw the game in the Windy City. Sheldon's squad was hailed as "a revelation of football speed and brains" by some observers, and one Chicago player was quoted as saying, "Give that Crimson team two weeks with their nose to the grindstone and the West will open its eyes."

In one of the best examples you'll ever read of someone watching IU football through Crimson-colored glasses, the *Daily Student* wrote, "With a machine that outplayed the champions of the West and only lost through hard luck, Indiana's chances for victories in the rest of her schedule are brighter than they've ever been."

It was an odd sentiment about an IU team that had just lost 28–0.

The loss to Chicago didn't completely derail the 1909 season. The Crimson went 3–2 the rest of the way and finished tied for fifth in the Western Conference with a 1–3 mark. But after the loss to the Maroons, something seemed to click in the Crimson on the defensive side of the ball that would set the tone for a brighter future. After giving up twenty-eight points to Chicago, Indiana allowed just twenty points the rest of the season and hammered Purdue 36–3.

In early December, the football team was celebrated as one of the best in school history, and a banquet was held in the team's honor at the Men's Gymnasium, which would later be known as the original Assembly Hall. The band and drum corps were on hand, as were food and cigars. But the real draw for the assembled crowd wasn't the eats or the smokes. It was the girls. Coeds were allowed at the affair, a fact that made it the most popular event of the month on campus.

"The girls have as much voice in the homage to be paid to the Crimson heroes as the men of the University," the *Daily Student* wrote.

Roughly a week after the banquet, the Crimson got the news they were hoping for. Sheldon would return as head coach for the 1910 season, but IU's director of athletics would not be around Bloomington for a while. He would spend the spring and summer in Chicago practicing law, and he would run the athletic department from a distance. The opening kickoff to the 1910 season at Jordan Field was filled with promise for the Crimson.

Before leaving, Sheldon announced that Berndt had been elected team captain for 1910, and he expected Berndt to provide leadership for the ball club during his absence. He also advised the Crimson to stay off the baseball diamond during the summer, and every player took an oath to "run whenever he saw a baseball from now on."

Sheldon couldn't afford to lose any more players. After all, he was certain 1910 was going to be everything 1909 wasn't.

When the 1909–10 school year finally came to a close in mid-June, the departing players had big plans for the summer. Halfback Harold King planned to prep for the football season by shoveling gravel during the last half of the summer term, ensuring that he would be in "good trim" by the fall. A player named Oakley planned to work on his physique by working in the hay fields "out west" during the summer months. Berndt, the Crimson' captain, wanted to take a different approach.

"What I need is a quiet place in the country with lots of time to rest and lots of milk to drink," Berndt told the *Daily Student*.

Three months later, Sheldon hit the ground running. He wasn't interested in the number of bodies that came out for practice. He didn't care about the enthusiasm on campus for his team. He had work to do, and he was going to wring everything he could out of his players.

At 10:00 a.m. on September 21, 1910, Sheldon assembled his team on Jordan Field and spent the first hour running drills with the ball. Another half hour was spent going over the new rules. The only eligible receivers would be the two ends, and they weren't allowed to catch a pass that was thrown more than twenty yards past the line of scrimmage. Passes could only be thrown by the quarterback, and he had to be at least five yards behind the line of scrimmage. All other players, save for the two ends, had to be at least one yard behind the line of scrimmage for a pass to be legal. On the defensive side of the ball, players were not allowed to leave their feet to make tackles. Diving was outlawed, as were "flying" tackles, which saw players just launch themselves sideways at ballcarriers. Under the new rules, a player making a tackle had to have at least one foot on the ground. On kickoffs and punts, meanwhile, the kicking team's players could not be blocked past the line of scrimmage until they had advanced twenty yards.

You can see why it took thirty minutes to explain the new rules.

The afternoon session was described as more "strenuous" and saw players working in more scrimmage situations. "The little coach realizes that he must have his men ready for hard work early," the September 22, 1910, *Daily Student* wrote. "To this end (he) has been doing his best to get them physically right. As soon as the men can stand it, he will send them into the hardest sort of workouts to master the new rules from the practical side. As it is now, he has them studying out all the possibilities of the revised style."

All but four starters were back from the 1909 team with only Paddock, Adam Leonard, Lloyd Sholty, and "Cy" Davis missing from the lineup. The first two graduated in the spring of 1910, and Sholty left to study medicine in Indianapolis. Davis, meanwhile, was sick, and the *Daily Student* oddly reported that he was "enjoying a siege of typhoid fever."

Indiana had four home games on its schedule, but the battle with Chicago would once again be held in the Windy City. Fan interest was once again sky high with more than two hundred fans showing up for every practice, including class registration day.

Sheldon was focused on the fundamentals, much to the surprise of his players and the students who watched the practice. They came out to Jordan Field to watch the team scrimmage, but instead they were treated to drill after drill.

"Most people would think Jimmie is doing it backwards," IU player "Cunny" Cunningham told the September 23, 1910, edition of the *Indiana Daily Student*. "I'll bet three-fourths of the coaches (at other schools) are working their men to death in an attempt to get into the new rules and the new plays. That isn't the thing. The fundamentals still hold no matter what the rules are, and players are still going to have to know how to tackle and fall on the ball and all that.... Sheldon is doing it the right way even if it does look to be backwards."

Despite the boring practices, the enthusiasm surrounding the team continued to build, so much so that the *Daily Student* felt the need to let a little air out of the team just a few days into practice.

"Great expectations sometimes bring great disappointments, and it is not wise to expect too much of a football team," the *Daily Student* wrote in late September. "Furthermore, Indiana University students as a rule are not much given to optimism. These two facts being noted, a third comes up. Either this University will boast of the greatest football eleven in its history this fall or there will be a wondrous amount of knocking on a bunch of fallen idols at the end of the season. One of these things is bound to come about."

Unlike in modern times, punts were one of the main ways teams tried to advance the ball.

Gill was one of the standouts in the early workouts, and he amazed the onlookers with his runs and ability to pull off "trick" plays during the practices. The only hiccup was the lack of a coach for the freshman team, and Sheldon was distracted by having to make calls and send telegrams to Chicago searching for someone to fill the job.

Just days before the season opener against DePauw at Jordan Field, however, Indiana looked to be in trouble. Injuries had decimated the squad, and several key players were hobbled. Frank Kimble, a guard on the team, was out with a severely sprained ankle, although he vowed to play even if he was on crutches at game time. Fullback Olice Winters had a wrenched shoulder. Halfback Harold King, after spending the summer shoveling gravel, could hardly walk thanks to his own sprained ankle. Two more players, Homer "Hercules" Dutter and Cloice Hatfield had ankle problems, and a number of other players were struggling with minor injuries.

Indiana would start the season at less than full strength, but the Crimson were ready to make a statement.

DEPAUW AT INDIANA * OCTOBER 2, 1910 * JORDAN FIELD

DePauw had not forgotten the whipping it took a year earlier, and the game with the Crimson was considered the biggest of the year for the fellas from

Greencastle. DePauw had hired a new head coach, and the optimism for the team, known as the Methodists at the time, was as high at DePauw as it was at Indiana.

Besides, DePauw accused the Crimson of playing "sissified" football. The *Greencastle Herald* claimed IU was an inferior team that had to resort to tricks to score wins. "It will be remembered that last year Indiana defeated DePauw by the repeated use of the forward pass," the paper wrote. "As far as straight football was concerned, she was on par if not better than the IU team."

Early on, it looked like the Herald might have a point. Dutter kicked off at precisely 3:00 p.m., and after a DePauw punt, IU's George Roberts fumbled after catching a pass. Indiana's defense held, and following another punt, Gill fumbled the ball away, giving DePauw the ball at the IU forty-yard line.

Again, Indiana's defense came up big. It forced a turnover when DePauw fumbled, and Frank Lindley scooped up the ball and scampered forty yards before being brought down. A twenty-yard run by Merrill Davis put the Crimson closer to the goal line, and three plays later, Berndt scored IU's first touchdown of the season when Gill found him with a pass, and Berndt scooted five yards into the end zone. Gill added the extra point—no easy feat considering the ball had to be kicked in a straight line from the spot where the TD was scored, creating some odd angles for conversions—to put IU up 6–0.

Another DePauw punt was followed by another Indiana fumble—ball security was an issue back in those days—and neither team managed to score through the end of the first quarter. It's important to note that time was not kept on a scoreboard as it is in modern football. Instead, teams agreed prior to game time how long halves would be, although halves were limited to a total of forty-five minutes on the clock, give or take a minute. That's not game time. That's forty-five minutes on the referee's watch, which means the first quarter ended at 3:23 p.m. The Crimson managed to score again in the second quarter when Davis went around the right end for a thirteen-yard touchdown run, and IU's extra point gave Indiana a 12–0 lead.

It was an edge that held up. DePauw only threatened in the closing minutes when a player named Overman returned a punt seventy yards, but Kimble tracked him down from behind, and the Methodists were limited to a field-goal attempt, which they missed. When the gun went off, the Crimson were 12–0 victors, and Sheldon was happy that he hadn't been forced to open his playbook. He only called simple plays, keeping IU's arsenal under wraps for the upcoming battle with Chicago.

It was a good thing, too. Maroons assistant coach Tom Kelley was in attendance at Jordan Field, and he returned to Chicago to tell Stagg that IU's size and shiftiness in the backfield would cause problems for his team. Stagg agreed, and he told reporters he was worried about the Crimson.

It was music to Sheldon's ears.

INDIANA AT CHICAGO * OCTOBER 8, 1910 * MARSHALL FIELD

Sheldon worked his team hard during the preseason, but those workouts were nothing compared to what he had in store for the Crimson in the days leading up to the Chicago game. The lights were brought back out to Jordan Field to let the team practice late into the evening, and a "ghost" ball, the white-painted pigskin, made its first appearance of the year. Spectators to the workouts saw a team that looked nothing like the Crimson squad that beat DePauw. Indiana's offense was completely different—by design.

More than two dozen plays were installed on Monday evening alone, and Sheldon was excited that he would have something new to throw at his alma mater. The weather, however, complicated things. The skies opened up for the next couple of days, turning Jordan Field—a notoriously slow-draining facility—into a quagmire. The Crimson weren't able to get much work done before they left for Chicago, and their final practice prior to the game was held at a beach on the shores of Lake Michigan following the long train ride north. In that workout, the Crimson didn't even work on plays. Sheldon knew full well that Stagg would have spies in the area, and he didn't want to give anything away.

Adding to the drama was the uncertainty about the status of Gill. Early in the week, the Crimson's halfback-punter-placekicker-defensive fullback received a telegram informing him that his mother had fallen ill at his home in Linton. Gill jumped on the earliest train back home straight from practice to be by his mother's side, and whether or not he could make it to Marshall Field hinged on the health of his mom.

Two days before the game, Thursday, October 6, Gill's mother underwent a procedure at noon to remove what was described as a "severe tumor." The surgery went well, and doctors told Gill he would be safe to head back to Bloomington. Early Friday morning Gill arrived back on campus, and shortly thereafter he boarded a train to Chicago along with his teammates, more than five hundred IU supporters, and prominent citizen George "Uncle Jake" Buskirk (whose family name now adorns the Buskirk-Chumley Theatre on Kirkwood Avenue).

Despite Gill's arrival, the *Daily Student* wasn't optimistic about how much he could help the Crimson. "It is hardly likely that he will be able to play his best game for the illness of his mother has been a great worry," the paper wrote. "Besides, he missed practice yesterday and has not scrimmaged since last Saturday."

The *Daily Student* was wrong.

In front of a crowd estimated at more than five thousand fans, Gill and the Crimson gave the Maroons everything they could handle. The first time he touched the ball, Gill picked up ten yards. On his first punt, he booted the ball fifty-five yards. With the game still scoreless late in the second quarter, Gill crushed a seventy-yard punt. That punt went into the end zone, however, and Gill was forced to kick the ball a second time (it was the rule at the time). Gill's second kick was returned twenty yards, and Chicago lined up for a field-goal attempt, its second of the game. Like the first, the Maroons' drop kick missed, and the teams went into halftime scoreless.

Defense ruled as the game remained scoreless late in the fourth quarter, but IU broke through when Cunningham found Berndt with a twenty-five-yard pass that put Indiana at the Chicago twelve-yard line. On the next play, Cunningham found Gill with another pass, and the sophomore bounded into the end zone for the first score of the game. He added the extra point to put Indiana up 6–0, and the Maroons were forced to punt on their next possession. IU kept Chicago pinned in its own territory for the rest of the game, and the final gun sounded with the Crimson walking off with their first-ever win over Stagg's club.

As the happy Crimson made their way back to Bloomington on their train from Chicago, the IU campus exploded in joy. Let's just say that if there was a Showalter Fountain at the time, the fish would have been in jeopardy. Bonfires sprung up everywhere, cigars were passed out, bands played, and more than one thousand people came out to the Student Building to celebrate. An impromptu parade broke out, and torch-carrying students made their way around campus, singing and dancing along the way.

With the Bloomington police acting as escorts, the students headed into town, and they wandered into a local playhouse. The booze flowed, and local businesses threw open their doors to join in the celebration. The procession, however, didn't cause any issues, and nobody was arrested in the chaos.

Two days later, with the team back in town, an event with the far-from-politically-correct name of "The Great Chicago Fire" saw another huge bonfire lit, and there was more dancing, singing, and speeches to mark the occasion. By the time the smoke cleared, Indiana's students were wiped out, but everyone was thrilled to have the much-sought-after win under their belts.

JAMES MILLIKIN AT INDIANA
* OCTOBER 15, 1910 * JORDAN FIELD

While the fans partied, Sheldon was focused on making sure his team didn't suffer a hangover at the level some of the students undoubtedly were sporting when the Crimson took on their next opponent, James Millikin University.

At a Jordan Field that was under repair—the rain softened the ground so badly the goal posts fell over—Sheldon pushed his team back to work the Monday after the Chicago game, and he pounded home the fact that Millikin was an unknown quantity. The university had been around for less than ten years at the time, and although it was thought Indiana would easily win, Sheldon was nervous about the game. His starters were nursing a number of aches and pains from the hard-fought Chicago game, and with a battle with Wisconsin looming, he didn't want his players to overlook Millikin.

Of course, that didn't stop Sheldon from bolting town.

The Friday before the game, Sheldon left the team in the hands of a pair of assistants and boarded a train bound for Champaign. With the Chicago game behind him, Sheldon was focused on Illinois, the only team he deemed a real threat to the Crimson's conference championship hopes. In those days, before coaching film or television, the only way to scout an opponent was to go watch them in person. It's not clear why Sheldon didn't send one of the assistants, but by the time kickoff arrived against Millikin, Sheldon was hundreds of miles away.

Not that he had to worry. Indiana scored in the first minute of play when Gill scored on a run, and he added another touchdown a few minutes later. He added a third score later in the game, and IU emptied the bench to save the starters for the future. When officials fired the pistol to end the game, the Crimson were up 34–0, and Millikin didn't come close to scoring. Indiana was 3–0 for the second time in its history, and it had outscored its opponents 52–0.

WISCONSIN VERSUS INDIANA
* OCTOBER 22, 1910 * WASHINGTON PARK

Although Indiana's official records list the Crimson as having played a road game at Wisconsin in 1910, that isn't the case. In fact, the Crimson battle with Wisconsin took on the air of a special occasion thanks to some Indianapolis businessmen.

The Crimson and the Badgers alternated the locations of their games, with Wisconsin hosting one year and Indiana the next. IU played in Madison during the 1909 season. The 1910 game was considered an opportunity for Indianapolis-based alumni to see the Crimson in person, and the game was moved from Bloomington to a larger stadium in Indy. Wisconsin didn't really care whether the game was played in Bloomington or Indianapolis, but the lure of a larger turnout—and therefore higher gate receipts—made the Badgers amenable to the change.

The railways saw an opportunity to make some extra money as well, and as the Crimson practiced at Jordan Field early in the week, the Indianapolis Southern Railroad announced a pair of special trains that would run from Bloomington to Indy the day of the game. The IU band would be on one of the trains, and the drum corps would take the other, giving the entire excursion the feeling of being an event.

The players would enjoy a special bonus. H. O. Smith of the Premier Motor Manufacturing Company agreed to furnish enough cars to take IU's players from the train station to their Indianapolis hotel when they arrived in town Friday, and the same cars would ferry the athletes to the stadium for the game Saturday. The Crimson would play Wisconsin at Washington Park, a baseball field that was home to the Indianapolis Indians at the time (it would later become the current site of the Indianapolis Zoo).

The week leading up to the battle with the Badgers was unseasonably warm, and with the season in full swing, Sheldon didn't want to push his players too hard. Practices were held in the evening, and the lights were brought out once again. Indiana knew it would face a challenge in playing UW thanks to the size of the Badger line, which impressed an IU assistant who had been dispatched to watch Wisconsin's previous game.

In front of a massive crowd at Washington Park, the Crimson got an early scare when the Badgers became the first team to score on them all season. The Badgers cracked the scoreboard first when a UW player named Burch split the uprights with a drop-kick to give Wisconsin a 3–0 lead. Indiana went into the second quarter still trailing for the first time all season, but the Crimson's work with the forward pass started to pay off in the second period.

A series of short passes helped Indiana move the ball down the field and put Wisconsin on its heels, and Olice Winter finished off the drive with a one-yard touchdown run. Gill added the extra point to put Indiana up 6–3 and ease the fears of some of the Crimson faithful.

Gill broke the game open late in the second quarter. Let's let the *Daily Student* tell the story.

"Near the end of the second quarter [Gill] pulled off the greatest play of the day, and one that will probably stand as the best of the season," the *Daily Student* reported. "He received a punt from Pierce on the fifty-five-yard line" (editor's note: that's not a typo; remember, the field was 110 yards long) "and ran through the entire Wisconsin eleven for the second touchdown. Practically every Badger had a shot at him, but they all rolled off like water from a duck's back. His dodging was something wonderful."

Gill once again added the extra point, and IU went up 12–3. It was all the Crimson would need. Indiana's defense forced Wisconsin to punt time and time again, and in the strategy of the time, the Crimson kept punting the ball right back to the Badgers on first down to drive them deeper and deeper into their own territory. Indiana did have an opportunity to score again in the second half, but three field-goal attempts by Gill missed.

Still, Indiana walked away a 12–3 winner to move to 4–0 on the season, much to the delight of the Indiana fans in attendance. The train cars were a merry place on the ride back to Bloomington that night, but the partiers couldn't have imagined they had witnessed something that wouldn't be seen at IU for more than half a century.

Indiana wouldn't open a football season 4–0 again until 1967.

BUTLER AT INDIANA * OCTOBER 29, 1910 * JORDAN FIELD

Indiana's next opponent was Butler, a team that put absolutely no fear into the Crimson. In contrast with the Millikin game earlier in the season when Sheldon made sure his team wasn't overlooking its next opponent, IU's coach didn't make any pretense about the Bulldogs. The Crimson practiced lightly all week, and when Friday rolled around, Sheldon again headed out of town, this time to West Lafayette to watch Purdue take on Illinois. The coaching of the team for the Butler game was again left to the assistants.

But there was an extra wrinkle this time around. Not only did Sheldon skip the game, he took Gill and Cotton Berndt along with him on the scouting trip. Sheldon put so much stock in the upcoming Illinois game—a homecoming game and the battle that could very well decide the 1910 Western Conference champion—that he robbed his team of its two best players to scout an opponent. In this day and age, it is a mind-boggling strategy, but for 1910, it was par for the course.

It also turned out that the stars weren't needed. Indiana piled up thirty-three points in the first half alone, scoring two touchdowns in the first quarter and four more in the second. Despite the fact that IU pulled its starters at halftime, Butler still couldn't crack the end zone and never really threatened. The 33–0 final, however, was seen as somewhat of a disappointment, considering Wabash had hung forty-eight points on Butler earlier in the season, and IU fans were warned that the Wabash faithful might get chatty after the game.

One of the most notable items about the Butler game was the fact that Cunny Cunningham rested the final five minutes of the game. Prior to the Butler blowout, Cunningham had played ten full games without missing a minute of action. Since the end of the 1909 DePauw game, Cunningham had played every snap of the Crimson' games against Chicago, Lake Forest, Wisconsin, Saint Louis, Illinois, Purdue, DePauw, Chicago again, Millikin, and Wisconsin again. He didn't miss a play along the way, another mind-blowing fact.

ILLINOIS AT INDIANA * NOVEMBER 5, 1910 * JORDAN FIELD

"And then—and then—well, the fight is on," the *Daily Student* opined following the Butler game. "All of the practice games and the monkey business is out of the way now, and Illinois comes next Saturday. The real big game of the season, in the light of past events, is scheduled for next Saturday afternoon on Jordan Field at whatever o'clock the officials may decide. Indiana will be ready in every way for the hardest game in years."

Despite the fact he had obviously had this game circled on his calendar since the start of the season, Sheldon tried to act as if Illinois was just another game once the week finally arrived. He made no changes to his practice schedule, working the players hard Monday through Thursday, and Friday saw a letup. The Crimson were relatively healthy, although Kimble had been bitten by a Butler player the previous week, and Gill and Berndt were fresh after taking a week off.

Around the team, however, it was clear that it wasn't a typical week. The sound of hammers accompanied the noise of whistles at practice as Indiana worked to finish the addition of more bleachers to Jordan Field. Tickets were selling briskly, and Illinois's supporters had bought tickets for every seat on the north side of the stadium. As of Tuesday more than three thousand tickets had been sold—a staggering number so early in the week during a time in which walk-up sales were the norm.

By Wednesday the pressure was starting to get to Sheldon, and he canceled a freshman game against the varsity second-string players that had been slated for 3:00 p.m. at Jordan Field, and he closed practice to the public. Anybody caught peeking into the stadium was quickly shooed away, and students were warned to keep a close eye out for anybody who didn't look like they belonged on campus.

Wednesday also brought the first sign of what would become a running story long after the game ended. It started to drizzle during practice, and Sheldon believed the cool weather would allow his players to work a bit harder. He closed the practice with wind sprints, which the *Daily Student* described as "the frightful foe of fat fellows," and he felt confident that his Crimson were ready.

Meanwhile, in Champaign, Illinois, the players were being driven harder than at any point in the season. Three-hour practices were the norm for the afternoon, and two more hours of signal practice were held in the armory at night. Its fans were excited as well. Two trains were scheduled to run to Bloomington bringing an estimated two thousand Illini fans with them.

Thursday in Bloomington saw the rain continue as the Crimson turned in their final strenuous workout, and water continued to pelt Jordan Field on Friday as well. Even as alumni started to arrive in Bloomington to enjoy homecoming festivities, there was concern that the condition of the field could have an impact on the game. Although Illinois—which the *Daily Student* inexplicably nicknamed "The Suckers"—weighed on average six pounds more than the Crimson, IU fans believed Indiana's speed would make the difference. A wet field, however, could change all that.

Lloyd Sholty, the Crimson starter who left the football team to go to medical school in Indianapolis prior to the start of the season, showed up in Bloomington, but he wasn't there for a visit. Sheldon gave the senior a uniform, and despite the fact he hadn't practiced all season, Sholty was put on notice that if the Crimson needed a substitute, his would be the first name called.

As kickoff time approached, however, Sheldon told Sholty he wouldn't be serving as a backup. He would be starting. And when the two teams lined up at 2:23 p.m. under cloudy skies, Sholty was on the field, ready to go back to battle. He made his presence felt on the defensive side of the ball immediately. After an IU punt, Sholty made the tackle on the return. Then on first down, he stopped an Illinois runner at the line of scrimmage. On second down, he plastered the ballcarrier again for no gain, forcing a punt.

Neither team could gain much traction with the ball, although the Jordan Field surface was holding up nicely. The field wasn't a muddy mess, but it was soft, limiting some of the Crimson cuts. The game was scoreless after the first quarter, and the defensive battle saw neither squad come within twenty-five yards of the goal line as the gun sounded to close the first half.

Sawdust was spread on the field during intermission to try to soak up some of the remaining moisture, but the presence of the bands on the field limited its effectiveness. Both offenses were limited in their effectiveness, as well, until the Crimson started to get something going midway through the third quarter. After Indiana turned the ball over on downs at the Illinois thirty-yard line, the Illini tried to gain ground by punting the ball on first down. Illinois shanked the kick, however, and it went just fifteen yards. Cunningham then gained back that distance and more when he found Berndt with a pass, giving the Crimson the ball at the Illinois twenty-six. Dutter and Cunningham both were stopped at the line of scrimmage on successive runs, and Gill lined up for a drop kick that could break the tie.

Gill missed, however, partially thanks to some shaky footing, keeping the game scoreless. IU again threatened late in the third quarter when Indiana drove to the Illinois twenty-five-yard line. While Crimson fans sang "It Looks Like a Bonfire Tonight" from the stands, Sheldon and his team worked to come up with a play that could break the game open.

On the first play of the fourth quarter, Indiana threw an interception, ending the threat. The two teams tried to advance the ball via punts, and Illinois got its first big break of the game when a twenty-five-yard run around end by Chester Roberts gave the Illini the ball at midfield. Naturally, Illinois immediately punted, with QB Otto Seiler booting the ball forty-five yards to Gill. Gill was immediately swarmed under, and on first down IU punted the ball back. The exchange of possessions, however, resulted in a net of ten yards for the Illini, which means their strategy worked. Two plays later, Seiler drilled a drop kick from thirty-five yards out to give Illinois a 3–0 lead. Indiana didn't have an answer. The spirit was sucked out of the fans, and the Crimson offense failed to get anything going. Not that Illinois moved the ball, either. Seiler could only manage two more field-goal attempts, but he missed both of them.

When the time ran out, Indiana had lost 3–0, ending its chances of winning a Western Conference crown. Illinois fans celebrated in the bleachers while IU fans sobbed. Well, not all Indiana fans. IU's accountants were thrilled. Thanks to the more than five thousand tickets sold, the gate receipts were estimated to total more than $2,000, a hefty chunk of change for 1910 and more than double the amount IU earned from its game in Champaign twelve months earlier.

The money didn't matter to Sheldon or any of the players. All they knew is they had let a winnable game slip away, and despite the fact they still hadn't allowed an opponent to score a touchdown all season, they wouldn't finish the year undefeated. Sheldon's dream of a title was dead, and all of his preparation had gone for nothing.

PURDUE AT INDIANA * NOVEMBER 19, 1910 * STUART FIELD

To say the campus was deflated would be a massive understatement. The season had been a joy ride that everyone had been on board with, but the loss took all the fun out of the year. Even though Indiana had one game left on the schedule, against archrival Purdue no less, enthusiasm for the football team plummeted.

With the game being held in West Lafayette, a special train had been arranged to take IU supporters to the game. But whereas a few weeks earlier fans packed the tracks to head to the Wisconsin game in Indianapolis, there were major concerns that the trains would go virtually unused. Adding to the lack of excitement was the fact Purdue wasn't very good. The Boilermakers were in the throes of a 1–5 season, and Purdue had managed to score a total of nineteen points on the season. The Boilers' 14–6 win over DePauw the week after IU lost to Illinois—the Crimson enjoyed a bye week after the devastating defeat—was a bright spot and showed Purdue wasn't about to give up.

The Crimson continued to work hard on Jordan Field, but the team had lost its edge. Sheldon was still installing new plays and drilling the fundamentals, but the sense of urgency that gripped the Crimson throughout the season was gone. He had given his players Monday and Tuesday of game week off. Another game between the freshmen and the reserves was called off at the last minute, mainly because Sheldon wanted to keep his players healthy.

Despite all the hand-wringing about a possible lack of support for the Crimson against Purdue, a sizable crowd of spectators boarded the Purdue Special on Saturday at 8:00 a.m., and they were warmly greeted in West Lafayette.

At 2:25 p.m., the game kicked off in front of 4,214 fans with Sholty again in the lineup. Purdue punted on its first possession, and the Crimson wasted no time getting on the scoreboard. A thirty-yard pass to Davis was followed by a touchdown catch and run by Gill, and his extra point gave IU a 6–0 edge two minutes into the game.

Indiana continued to play fierce defense, and Purdue never threatened during the first half. IU went into halftime with a 6–0 lead, and a Gill dropkick early in the third quarter gave Indiana a 9–0 edge. The Boilermakers managed to drive to the Hoosier fifteen-yard line midway through the fourth quarter, and Purdue attempted a field goal from the twenty-five-yard line. That kick was blocked, however, and IU took over. Berndt picked up thirty yards on a run, and Roberts gained another thirty on a pass. Two plays later, Gill scored another touchdown, and his kick put Indiana up 15–0.

Indiana's defense made sure the score stayed that way. The season ended with Indiana's 15–0 victory, giving the Crimson a 6–1 record on the season and a 3–1 mark in the Western Conference, good enough for third place behind Illinois and Minnesota, who were deemed to be tied for the championship despite the fact Illinois was 4–0 in the league and Minnesota was just 2–0. Illinois outscored its opponents 89–0 on the year, and Minnesota finished 6–1 with its only loss coming to Michigan, a team that was not yet part of the Western Conference. Either way, Indiana was left out of the equation despite the fact it had allowed six points all season and did not allow an opponent to score a touchdown.

Indiana's greatest season to date ended as little more than an afterthought.

The Crimson saw left end Berndt, left guard Allen Messick, and right tackle Dutter land on the all-conference team, and fans were outraged that Gill had been snubbed. He joined Hatfield on the second-team all-conference squad. He also was selected to play an All-Star game against Washington University during the Christmas holidays, but conference rules prevented him from appearing in the game. Gill was, however, elected to be the captain of Indiana's 1911 team. Indiana's success on the field didn't ensure Sheldon's return. There was some speculation that he wouldn't be retained for the 1911 season due to his desire to go back to Chicago for the spring and summer once again, but in early December, it was announced that Sheldon would be back for at least one more season.

Oddly, after drenching the 1909 squad in honors and glory following that campaign, the same treatment wasn't afforded the 1910 team. The annual football banquet was held, but there was none of the pomp and circumstance that surrounded the previous season. With so many key players leaving—seven starters played their last game at Purdue—there wasn't the same buzz around the program.

Maybe it was justified. IU slumped to .500 in 1911, and the Crimson fell to 2–5 in 1912. Indiana failed to win a single conference game over those two seasons, and after going 3–4 overall and 2–4 in the league in 1913, Sheldon left Indiana for good. He headed back to Chicago and became an investment banker, leaving the game of football behind. Sheldon closed out his IU coaching career with a 35–26–3 record, which still ranks him fourth on IU's list of winningest coaches. He currently ranks third on IU's all-time win percentage list with a mark of .570. He died July 8, 1965, in LaPorte, Indiana, at the age of eighty-five.

Berndt, Indiana's captain in 1910, went on to become the head basketball coach at IU from 1913 to 1915, and he continued to work at IU after leaving coaching. He is the only IU athlete ever to serve as a captain of three sports at Indiana, and he served as mayor of Bloomington from 1935 to 1938. Berndt was elected to the IU Athletics Hall of Fame in 1997. He passed away at the age of sixty-three in July 1947.

Gill graduated from IU in 1912 and moved on to coaching football. He was the head coach at Lombard College in Illinois and Albion College in Michigan before taking over at North Dakota from 1914 to 1918. He became the head man at Kentucky for the 1918 and 1919 seasons, beating the Crimson in his first year at UK. In 1921 he took over as the head coach at Michigan City Elston (Indiana) High School, where he spent twenty-nine years in the job.

He retired in 1946, and he died of a heart attack March 8, 1947, in Daytona Beach, Florida. Gill was inducted into the Indiana Football Hall of Fame in 2007.

Indiana's feat of going a season without allowing an opposing touchdown will never be matched. Today's offenses are too high-powered, and the rules have tilted the playing field too much in the offense's favor for any defense to pull off a season shutout again. Although the game was much, much different more than one hundred years ago, Indiana fans can take pride in knowing that once upon a time, the Crimson boasted one of the most feared defenses around, one that shouldn't be forgotten.

ABOVE, FIGURE 4.1. George Frank "Duke" Trimble, shown on the far right with the 1908–9 basketball team, suffered a minor injury that eventually took his life. *IU Archives P0020328*

FACING, FIGURE 4.2. Arthur "Cotton" Berndt was captain of the football, baseball, and basketball teams during his time at IU and was a critical part of IU's powerful 1910 football team, which didn't allow a touchdown all season. *IU Archives P0020671*

"Cotton" Berndt Foot Ball Capt 1910

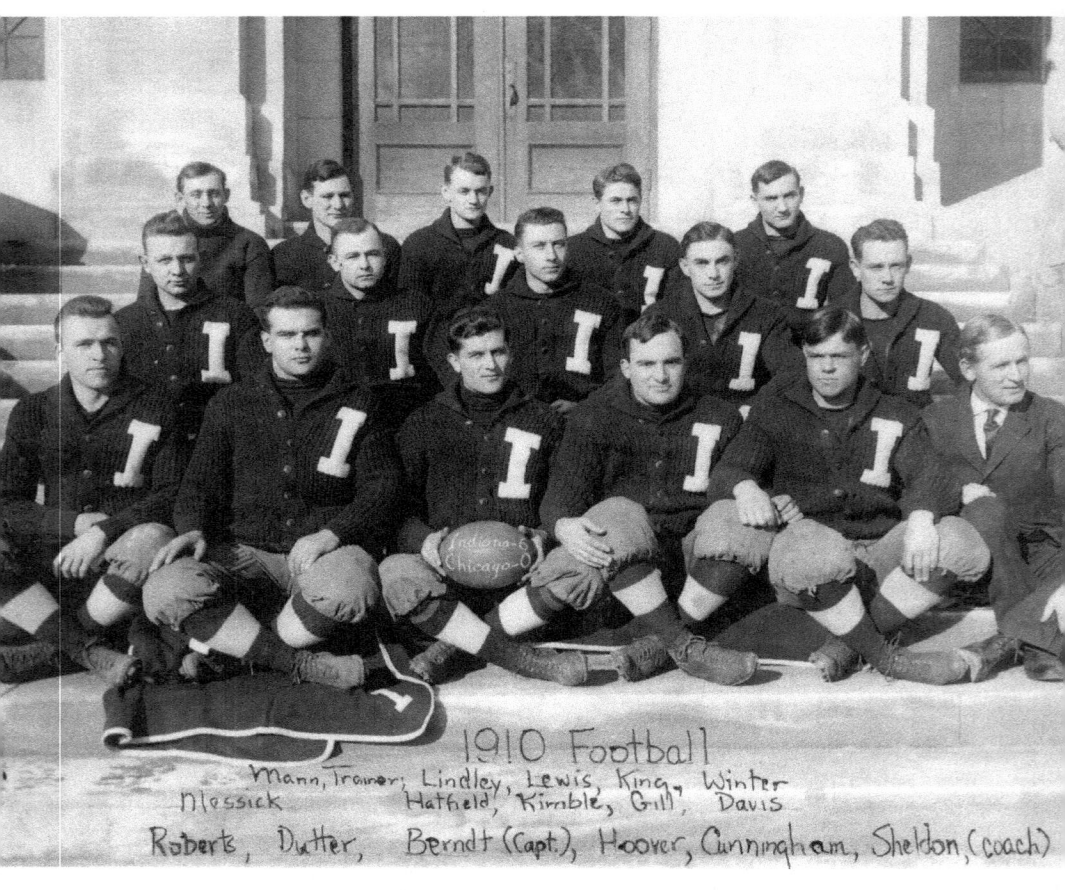

FIGURE 4.3. The 1910 football team. *IU Archives P0053063*

5

The Baseball Riot

If history teaches us anything, it's that things are never as bad as they seem. Usually, things are never as bad as they once were.

Take, for instance, the 2008–9 school year. Indiana's football and basketball programs were a lot less than fun to watch that season, and IU fans had little to cheer about. Then–head coach Bill Lynch led his football team, which was coming off an appearance in the Insight Bowl the season before, to just a 3–9 record overall. Indiana managed just one conference win. That lone 21–19 victory over Northwestern on homecoming was the highlight of a season that saw both a five-game losing streak and a four-game losing skid.

Over at Assembly Hall, new head coach Tom Crean didn't fare much better with his men's basketball squad. The once-proud program won four of its first six games but then picked up just two more victories the rest of the way en route to a 6–25 campaign. In conference play, IU managed to knock off Iowa 68–60 in early February to avoid the indignity of being shut out in the Big Ten, finishing the season with a 1–17 league mark.

The two programs combined to play forty-three games that school year, and they won only nine of them. Their combined Big Ten record was 2–24.

It was brutal. But it could have been worse. It had been worse.

Nearly one hundred years earlier, the Indiana faithful found even less to cheer about. IU athletics struggled mightily when it came to varsity sports, and the 1911–12 school year saw only one team—the basketball squad—win a conference game. Basketball went 1–9 during that year, while football went 0–3–1, and the baseball team lost all eight of its league outings.

Fortunes didn't get much better the next year. During the 1912–13 school year, the football and basketball programs combined to pull off a feat IU fans hope never, ever happens again. The two teams finished their respective seasons with zero conference wins between them and only seven total victories.

James Sheldon's football team went 2–5 overall, scoring wins over Franklin College and Washington University. But during play in the Big Ten's precursor, the Western Conference, IU went zero for five, losing to Chicago, Illinois, Iowa, Northwestern, and Purdue. Indiana was outscored 94–26 in league games, and the season marked the second straight year IU had gone winless in conference.

Over at Assembly Hall—the original Assembly Hall, then known as the Men's Gymnasium—head coach Arthur Powell led his team to a 5–1 record in nonconference games, but the Crimson took the collar in Western Conference games. IU went 0–10, falling twice to Purdue, Ohio State, Northwestern, Wisconsin and Illinois. Indiana closed the season with a 5–11 record.

Sixteen conference games, zero wins. During an era in which Indiana featured just three sports that played in a conference, baseball was the only shot left for the Crimson to gain any bragging rights in league play.

There wasn't a lot of enthusiasm that the team could pull it off, but a change of head coaches gave baseball at least some semblance of hope. Arthur "Cotton" Berndt was a former IU football star who took over as head baseball coach for the 1913 season. The team turned some heads by winning its season opener against the Indy Independents 2–0 April 14, 1913. Two days later, IU took on Illinois and lost its first conference game by a 9–5 mark. It seemed like business as usual for the Cream and Crimson, but Indiana showed some spark by scoring the first conference win of the season April 18, beating Iowa 4–2.

The victory gave IU athletics one win in conference play over three sports, matching the effort of the 1911–12 school year. Baseball was off to a 2–1 start, but nobody was willing to concede that the tide was turning for IU just yet.

Berndt's squad had nearly a week off before its next game, an April 24 battle with Wisconsin in Madison, but Indiana hit the road for a three-game trip that would see the Crimson play the Badgers and then travel to Beloit College for a game and, finally, to Chicago before returning home. IU's train left late in the evening April 23 following a practice that focused on improving the team's defense.

"The team is now taking on the appearance of a real machine," wrote the *Bloomington World*.

Berndt's machine proved its win over Iowa wasn't a fluke. Carl Schultz took the mound for the Crimson in Madison, and he baffled the Badgers all afternoon despite a lack of control.

"Pitcher Schultz, although a little wild at the beginning of the game, soon settled down," wrote the *Daily Student*. "Although issuing free transportation to seven batters, (Schultz) caused nine to smote holes in the atmosphere."

In other words, according to our 1913-to-twenty-first-century English-language translation book, Schultz walked seven batters but struck out nine en route to a 10–4 win over the Badgers in front of two thousand screaming Wisconsin fans.

The Crimson had their second conference win of the season, and they had every reason to celebrate. Little did they know the party was just getting started.

More than a century later, it's difficult to imagine the world of 1913. No radio. No television. No internet. No cell phones. Movie theaters were a novel option, but live theater was alive and well, as were various revues and variety shows. Beyond that, reading and social clubs were far and away the best entertainment options for the young and the restless on a college campus.

It also meant the smallest spark could turn into a major celebration. Parties and parades could pop up at the drop of a hat, and they often did.

Sometimes in Bloomington, all it took was the clicking of a telegraph.

Reporters from the *Indiana Student* filed their reports from Madison following the IU win, sending their story over telegraph wire. The story was received in Bloomington around 7:30 p.m. local time, and three minutes after those dots and dashes arrived with the results, all hell broke loose.

Word quickly spread that Indiana had won its second league game of the season, doubling the effort of the previous year. Students were roused at the news, and with nothing else to do on a Thursday night, a mob of several hundred formed to celebrate the win. A makeshift band was assembled, and, as mobs were wont to do in 1913, the band led the mob on a parade.

The parade marched through the library (the current Franklin Hall, next to the Sample Gates) and along the byways of what is now known as the Old Crescent. Then, as now, the strategy was to go where the girls were, so the cacophonous hoard headed through an area known as "sorority alley." Like a snowball rolling down hill—or maybe the Pied Piper working his way through town—students were recruited to join the party, and the growing group took a right to head west down Third Street.

The parade finally headed north toward the Library before turning back west to its intended destination—Kirkwood Avenue. Kirkwood is the main thoroughfare in Bloomington, the heart of the action in the city, and it was back in 1913 as well. Not content to stay on the street, the mob saw the doors to the Crescent Theatre, and there was nobody to stop them from entering the building. Students headed into the theater and disrupted the show, and the orchestra played a song only described as "Indiana." Parade participants and the people in the seats cheered the baseball nine, and they literally sang the praises of Schultz.

Bored with the Crescent, the parade headed back on the street and moved to the Rex Theatre. There, the theater manager—identified only as Sanford—refused entrance to the parade, citing safety concerns because the house was filled with women and children. Bloomington police officers had noticed the mob—mainly because it was impossible to miss them—and blocked the doors.

Undeterred, the parade continued up Kirkwood to Walnut, where it turned north and moved to the Harris Grand Theatre on the corner of Seventh and Walnut. The theater manager at the Harris Grand tried the same tactic that was used at the Rex, claiming that he couldn't open the doors because he already had a full house and was worried about the safety of his patrons. Denied once, the mob would not be denied a second time.

Ignoring the requests to stay out, students pushed their way into the theater anyway, and the parade rushed into the building. Confusion reigned inside the Harris as patrons wondered what was going on. Some students stormed the stage, and some of the audience members who had been watching the show decided it was time to go. They headed for the exits as the parade was forcing itself in, and a full-on panic was brewing.

A theater carpenter decided he needed to clear the front of the theater, and he shoved a student off the stage into the first row of seats. The student landed on some seats and was slightly injured. Meanwhile, people crowded the aisle, and the situation crossed the line from scary to downright dangerous when a woman dropped her baby amid the stomping legs of the mob. Thankfully, the baby was recovered uninjured.

Outside the theater, parade participants who couldn't push their way into the Harris Grand headed back toward the Main Square and, using stolen signs from the Rex, provided the element that turns a rowdy parade into a riot. Bonfires sprang up on every corner of the Square despite the best efforts of the police, who started to get physical with members of the mob. Each time a fire was put out, another would pop up in its place.

Police Chief Joseph B. Hensley, remembering a street corner demonstration two years earlier that featured fires that damaged the brick streets, ordered his men to do whatever it took to put the fires out. Fire Chief William Shinn failed to help matters when he refused to call in his troops to put out the fires because he was worried his hoses would be cut.

With no help from the fire department, police officers responded with physical force. A number of melees broke out, and what was described as "one prominent student" went down with an injured arm. Several officers then picked out one student and focused their wrath upon him, and, according to the *Bloomington World*, "the glitter of drawn revolvers added the necessary local color." Following a short fight, the student was arrested and shuttled into a nearby building. His fellow classmates were worried about what was going on behind closed doors, but they couldn't get into the building, thanks to the presence of a local man, Charles Carter, who had been deputized for the night and was holding the crowd at bay with a loaded revolver.

As the riot started to dissipate a bit, the arrested student was taken to the nearby police headquarters and charged with rioting. Some of his friends showed their displeasure with the police action by bombarding the police station with rocks, and a window was shattered along the way.

Three hours after the celebration-turned-riot had begun, it was all but wrapped up. But not completely. A fight broke out near the Indiana Café, and a car belonging to café manager Ralph Sours was damaged. Also damaged was sophomore Karl Battenburg, who took the brunt of a beating. The police intervened and went on a chase for roughly twenty assailants, but they got away.

The next afternoon, local businessmen met with IU President William Lowe Bryan to discuss the incident and come up with a plan to avoid such demonstrations in the future. That same afternoon, a completely unaware IU baseball team knocked off Beloit 2–1 in a seven-inning game that was shortened by rain.

The Indiana baseball team would go on to post an 11–4 record that season overall and a 6–3 record in conference play, good enough to land them in third place. Luckily for IU and the city of Bloomington, the third conference win of the season, a 5–4 victory over Wisconsin on May 3, didn't result in the same outpouring of dangerous enthusiasm.

Indiana would never again suffer through such rough times in its various athletics, although student riots have not been uncommon in the wake of major victories. But IU's first athletics-based riot showed some of the enthusiasm fans had for the Cream and Crimson. Although that excitement was misplaced, it shouldn't be forgotten.

FIGURE 5.1. The 1913 baseball team, whose victories incited a wild night in Bloomington. *IU Archives P0022122*

STUDENTS ENGAGE IN A NEAR-RIOT.

Build Fires on Brick Streets and are Arrested.

A hilarious celebration by the students last night following the victory of the Indiana baseball team over Wisconsin, almost culminated in serious trouble with the police and one student was arrested as a ring leader. Policeman Dudley was struck on the head with a big goods

FIGURE 5.2. A headline from the April 25, 1913, *Bloomington Telephone* announces the downtown trouble started by the 1913 baseball team. *IU Archives*

6

Money Problems and a Massive Improvement

You can judge the importance of money by all the little sayings that have been made up surrounding currency.

"You have to spend money to make money."

"Money doesn't grow on trees."

"You get what you pay for."

"The love of money is the root of all evil."

You could have come up with those off the top of your head. The story of IU athletics over the years has been one of financial struggle. The challenge of drawing fans to games and filling the coffers of the athletic department has long been an issue, and it had nothing to do with the product on the field or hardwood.

Until IU moved its athletic complex to the north side of Seventeenth Street in 1960, Indiana played its games right in the center of campus. Whether it was at Jordan Field or the multiple Men's Gymnasiums or the original Memorial Stadium, fans faced issues getting to the games.

Bloomington is the quintessential college town, a place with a large school in a location with a small-town feel. It's one of IU's biggest strengths.

And one of the university's biggest weaknesses is the fact that Bloomington is the quintessential college town, a place with a large school in a location with a small-town feel.

That means that for the majority of IU's athletic history, there weren't major highways leading to Bloomington. Once in town, visitors had to follow two-lane roads through neighborhoods to get to games, and then they had to park whatever transportation they used in a grassy field or on side roads.

God forbid it should rain.

Fans could take trains, but there still was a distance to cover between the train stations and the stadium or arena. And in the early years, cars weren't nearly as reliable or comfortable as they would become.

In other words, filling the stands has always been a challenge, and the support of students and Bloomington residents was critical to the financial success or failure of the athletic programs. The establishment of the Big Ten Network in 2007 has more than doubled the operating budget of IU's athletic department, and the results of the faucet of money being turned on can be seen at Memorial Stadium, Simon Skjodt Assembly Hall, Cook Hall, Bart Kaufman Field, Andy Mohr Field, and the pile of other improvements in facilities over the past decade.

But money woes have long been an issue at IU, and on more than one occasion, the future of the athletic programs in Bloomington hinged on luck and the foresight to avoid an unwise decision.

Halloween of 1903 was one of the darkest days in IU's athletics history.

Indiana was slated to play Purdue for the annual state championship, and for the first time ever, the game would be played at neutral site in Indianapolis's Washington Park. A massive crowd was expected, and four trains were chartered to carry thousands of fans to the game. Two trains on the Cleveland, Cincinnati, Chicago, and St. Louis Railway would travel to the game from Lafayette, and two trains on the Chicago, Indianapolis, and Louisville Railway—better known as the Monon Railroad—would carry fans from Bloomington.

More than one thousand fans arrived safely from Bloomington for the 2:45 p.m. kickoff, but tragically, the same couldn't be said of the trains coming from Purdue.

The Cleveland, Cincinnati, Chicago, and St. Louis Railway, also known as the "Big Four" Railway, provided a mixture of older wooden coaches and steel cars. The Purdue team rode in the cars at the front of the procession. As the trains sped into the city of limits of Indianapolis, a coal train was on the same track, headed the opposite direction. A signaling error had left the two trains on a collision course, and by the time the conductor of the Purdue train saw the coal train barreling toward him, it was too late. He threw on his air brakes and jumped out of the engine.

The passengers on the train had nowhere to go.

The massive crash destroyed the wooden cars at the front of the train, and it knocked a number of other cars off the tracks. In all, seventeen people, including fourteen Purdue players, two assistant coaches, and the team trainer, were killed, and fifty others were injured.

One player, Purdue's Harry Leslie, was pronounced dead at the scene and taken to the morgue. The captain of both the football and the baseball team at Purdue lay among the dead until morticians prepped his body to be embalmed, at which point they discovered he had a pulse. Leslie was rushed to the hospital, and after undergoing several operations and weeks of recovery, he eventually recovered, although he would need a cane for the rest of his life. Leslie later earned a law degree and became first speaker of the house for the Indiana House of Representatives, and later he became governor of the state of Indiana from 1929 to 1933.

The game, which was irrelevant in light of the tragedy, was called off.

That triggered another tragedy, one that could have killed Indiana athletics.

One of the reasons IU agreed to play the game in Indianapolis was that a larger crowd could be seated at Washington Park than at Jordan Field in Bloomington, and the game was poised to rescue Indiana athletics from financial ruin. No game, however, meant no gate receipts, and the situation was beyond dire for IU.

As the public mourned the dead in the days following the wreck, the treasurers of the two athletic associations from Purdue and Indiana met in Indianapolis to go over the financial impact. Purdue had expenses of $600 that were supposed to be covered by IU, but Director of Athletics James Horne made it clear that without the game receipts, the Indiana Athletic Association couldn't reimburse Purdue immediately.

IU didn't have the $500 it needed to provide an advance to an assistant coach who was considering leaving for another job. An upcoming game against Illinois was sure to cost IU another $500 in expenses, and there was fear that the football season would have to be canceled.

"The statements of Coach Horne this morning on the financial outlook of athletics at Indiana should make it clear to everyone connected with the University that our athletic finances are in such a shape that it will be a long time before they can be put on a basis of solvency," stated the November 4, 1903, *Daily Student*. "According to Mr. Horne, we are $2,000 in debt with absolutely no assets, except the football outfits and a small amount of other paraphernalia. Plainly speaking, we are almost bankrupt."

The football team's training table was immediately discontinued, and students were asked to donate money to buy the football team letterman sweaters.

It was clearer than ever that IU athletics were barely getting by. The only revenue generated by the athletic department came from ticket sales, donations, solicitations from local merchants, and regular fund-raising efforts and shows. Horne suggested increasing ticket prices. IU was falling behind its Big Nine brethren thanks to financial issues, and keeping up with the Joneses was critical to the future success of IU athletics.

The 1903 football team incurred total expenses of $5,100.06 compared with revenues of $3,557.00, a deficit of $1,543.06. IU students didn't feel a sense of urgency to help out, contributing a total of $79.95 toward filling the gap.

So dire were the financial issues that Horne contemplated an unthinkable decision—field an indoor track team or the basketball team. He couldn't do both, and basketball, in particular, lost money faster than the football team.

It's not clear what kind of arrangement was made or how the department limped on—possibly with help from the university, considering the administration's reticence to help out in the future—but the basketball team did play in 1904 as scheduled.

Despite the financial turmoil, the 1904 football team went 6–4 under Horne, but the need for more money inspired forty students and ten faculty members to form a new Athletic Association that could help solve some of the problems through better organization.

Even IU president William Lowe Bryan weighed in.

"The athletic interests of Indiana needs funds," Bryan wrote. "To provide sufficient amounts to the Association is a necessity. Students who have watched athletic developments here for several years express themselves as confident that the thing in which Indiana is deficient is the lack of organized support given to teams."

Horne, meanwhile, was in no condition to continue as coach of the football team. In 1903, Horne was with the track team prepping for an indoor meet in Louisville when he demonstrated the twelve-pound hammer throw for a group. Horne showed off his technique and let fly, but he lost his direction, and his hammer throw went awry.

Roughly 150 feet away, Bruce Lockridge—the starting end for the football team, the captain of the track team, and president of the Athletic Association—was working with the discus throwers. Hearing shouts of warning, Lockridge looked up and took the twelve-pound hammer in the head. His skull was crushed, and he died two hours later.

Horne, naturally, was destroyed emotionally, and contemporary accounts report that Horne attempted to take his own life in his grief. What is certain is that Horne was prone to illness after the incident, and he was judged unable to remain in his position for the 1905–6 school year.

That meant IU went into the fall sports season of 1905 without an official coach for the football or basketball team, and there was no director of athletics. President Bryan encouraged the Athletic Association to run itself as a business, with all focus on finishing the year in the black, and he warned IU would not be on the hook for any overages. He also wouldn't help with hiring a new coach.

"As an individual, I have no authority from the board of trustees to employ a football coach," Bryan wrote to the Athletics Association in a letter from the IU Archives.

Enter James Sheldon, a Chicago lawyer and former player for Amos Alonzo Stagg at the University of Chicago, who was first introduced in chapter 4. Sheldon took over as football coach, and, working with Zora Clevenger, an IU alumnus who served as bookkeeper and baseball coach in 1905–6, he ensured the Athletic Association turned a slight profit.

Still, in December of that year, President Bryan held a dinner for thirteen lettermen and members of the Athletic Association Board of Control, where he made it clear the university would not assume any financial responsibility for athletics in the future.

Money continued to be an issue, although IU would occasionally enjoy a windfall that gave the Athletic Association a bit of breathing room. For instance, the 1908 IU-Purdue football game, back from a one-year hiatus triggered by a dispute over the medical school, drew seven thousand fans to West Lafayette, more than a few of whom were more concerned with the point spread than the actual outcome. Regardless, IU cleared $1,750 in that game, giving the programs a boost.

The Athletic Association ran on a shoestring budget for the next few years, clearing $150 in profit in the 1909–10 school year before running slight deficits for a couple of years. That led to less-than-impressive investments in facilities such as Jordan Field, and IU fell behind its conference rivals in that area.

The overall financial struggles and general mediocrity of IU's athletics teams in the early 1910s became an issue that reached President Bryan's office. Bryan expected a certain level of excellence at IU, and Indiana sports were not meeting that standard. Simply put, IU's struggles were becoming a measure of embarrassment for the school.

In late 1914, Bryan proposed a conference of faculty, students, and alumni to discuss IU's athletics situation and try to come up with a plan to take IU to a successful future.

Students and alumni had made suggestions, and it was time for the university to listen.

Indiana's facilities were serviceable, but that doesn't mean they were impressive. For all its charm, the Men's Gymnasium wasn't exactly built with basketball in mind. IU students weren't thrilled with the conditions of the building, and they weren't shy about complaining to the faculty about the state of athletics in Bloomington.

IU suffered a 19–11 home loss to Earlham on January 24, 1914, the fourth straight loss to open the season. On the heels of a 1912–13 campaign that saw the Crimson go 5–11 overall and 0–10 in the Big Nine, the students decided one of the reasons for the team's struggles was a lack of proper facilities. The day after the loss to Earlham, a meeting of fifteen students and prominent alumni was held, and five temporary committees were appointed to get the ball rolling toward a new facility. A mass meeting was called January 28 to involve more students, and prominent faculty members and some alumni from Indianapolis were asked to speak.

George M. Cook, the president of the Indianapolis alumni association, was the main speaker, but Judge Charles Hepburn of the IU School of Law was on hand to speak, as was student speaker Albert Stump, who appears time and again throughout the early history of IU athletic facilities. Two petitions were drawn up—one for the students and one for the alumni—to be circulated.

The student version centered on the idea that a gymnasium could help the men and women currently on campus develop their bodies as well as their minds. They laid out five reasons for a new gym in their petition.

> We, the undersigned, students in Indiana University herein petition the trustees of said university that the next building built from the funds derived from the tax for the use of the University be a Men's Gymnasium.
>
> First, because the present gymnasium is totally inadequate for the present and future needs of the students of the university.
>
> Second, because the gymnasium now in use is unsanitary, which condition has not nor cannot be improved by ordinary methods of sanitation.
>
> Third, because we believe that Indiana University is handicapped under the existing conditions in its attempts to meet the physical needs and requirements of the students.
>
> Fourth, because we believe that the physical needs of the men of Indiana must be fully met as must the mental needs if Indiana is to class itself under the head of "university."
>
> Fifth, because at the present time Indiana University is far behind the state universities in the middle west in the matter of gymnasium and physical training equipment.

The alumni, meanwhile, took a different, broader approach that focused not only on how a new gymnasium could help develop students but also—and this is key—how it could help IU keep up with other institutions in terms of recruiting.

> *To the Board of Trustees of Indiana University:*
>
> We, the undersigned, alumni of Indiana University, respectfully petition that you use the first available funds for the construction of a new gymnasium.
>
> We feel that a new and adequate gymnasium is Indiana's first and most pressing need. Our reasons for this conviction are:
>
> 1. That the present gymnasium is altogether inadequate to meet the need of general physical training for the men of the University.
> 2. That Indiana University is not on a parity with other Universities of the conference in facilities for physical training and athletics; that with the present physical equipment, instead of our attracting men to our institution, they are going to schools better equipped.

> 3. That the continued inferiority of Indiana's athletic teams is in a large measure attributable to present conditions, which render year-round physical training and development impossible.
> 4. That the present structure cannot be altered to afford satisfactory accommodations, and that any attempt at alteration would be unsatisfactory and unprofitable.
>
> This, in brief, is our reason for petitioning you to vote for A NEW GYMNASIUM FIRST FOR A GREATER INDIANA."

Point 2, of course, is no different than the decision to build a new practice facility outside the current Assembly Hall and construct the North and South End Zone facilities at Memorial Stadium. Those buildings were designed to help recruiting, and, to a certain extent, point 2 makes the same argument for a new gym.

In any case, the student petition was placed on file at the front desk of the library, where it was signed by more than five hundred students. The alumni petition, meanwhile, was circulated to alumni associations both in and out of state. Letters poured in from alumni wishing the students success in their efforts, and members of the board of trustees were inundated with letters supporting the construction of a new gymnasium.

The chairman of the Central Committee, which was made up of the chairmen of the five committees that had been formed January 25, was Jack Horner, who seems to have been on the alumni side of things. Horner admitted in the March 17, 1914, edition of the *Daily Student* that the Central Committee wasn't looking to sway the board of trustees with facts. Instead, it was looking to appeal to their emotions without angering anyone. He said:

> The six or eight men who will appear before the Trustees next Tuesday will have no statistics prepared. We have collected no statistics regarding the gymnasium, feeling that the need of a new one is sufficiently evident without that. The committee all during the movement for a new gymnasium has tended to refrain from using any methods or material which would be antagonistic to those who oppose the proposition. We have had the opportunity to bring forces to bear which would have been more strenuous in results but have refrained because the committee has not met with sufficiently open opposition to warrant such.

Horner cited the reactions of the players at the recently completed IHSAA State Basketball Tournament as proof that something had to be done.

"High school students who were here attending the basketball tournament asked such questions as, 'Isn't this a temporary place that you are using for the tournament?'" Horner complained to the *Daily Student*. "They seemed to turn their noses at the sight of the structure. They are the young people from whom the coming students of Indiana University will be drawn, and if the trustees vote to appropriate funds for a new gymnasium Indiana will stand a much better chance of getting more and better students from these high schools."

Horner and his committee went in front of the board of trustees on March 24, and the board seemed intrigued, if noncommittal. One trustee, Judge Joseph Hooker Shea, put forward a motion to order President Bryan to investigate the plans and cost of constructing a new gymnasium. The motion passed, but the trustees made no promises to the students or alumni. All they would commit to was to discuss the matter again at their next meeting in June, when the annual budget would be discussed. It was reported in the *Daily Student* in April, however, that the president of the board of trustees, Senator Benjamin Shively, did say that the construction of a new gymnasium in the next two years "was not at all an improbability."

Not everyone, however, was excited about the idea. Trustee Theodore Rose questioned how the Central Committee could ask for as much as $100,000 to build a gymnasium when "people all over the state were hollering for vocational education." Despite Rose's reticence, the trustees still seemed to favor building a new gym in the near future.

June came and went without any news of a new gymnasium, but the students were patient. Finally, during a board meeting on December 2, 1914—it was actually the same day the Collegiate Basketball Rules Committee defined charging and blocking fouls—the gym came one step closer to reality.

In a "Statement of Needs" presented to the Governor and Legislative visiting committee, the board—oddly, on the motion of the aforementioned Rose—included the need of a "gymnasium or Physical Culture addition to the Student Building" among its requirements for the future. The board was rather blunt in its assessment of the physical state of the student body:

> It is needed by all the men of the university; not only those who take part in athletics, but still more by the hundreds and thousands who do not take part in athletics. Our University physician finds that very many of the entering freshmen are distinctly defective in their physical development. He has

prescribed corrective gymnastics for large numbers of them. Success in this direction means far greater success in the intellectual work of the students and also in the work which they will do after they leave the University. We have no adequate men's gymnasium at present and the Trustees wish to supply this need at the earliest possible time.

The idea of adding to the Student Building was wildly unpopular at the time and never was seriously considered. Still, the board managed to drag its feet a little longer, and the students started to get restless.

With Europe falling ever deeper into what would eventually become known as World War I, the students issued a petition asking for the faculty's consent to establish a military battalion on campus. The battalion would consist of four companies totaling four hundred to six hundred men, with the government providing free guns, clothes, and overcoats. The battalion would draw $4,000 over thirty-six weeks from the US government, and it was pointed out that the $4,000 could simply be put in the university's general fund.

Oh, and the US War Department just happened to encourage the construction of an Armory for the battalion, and, hey, that Armory could be used as a gymnasium! How about that?

The administration wasn't impressed with the petition that was distributed, and it saw the idea as nothing but a ham-handed way for the students to backdoor their way into a gym.

"There was also a feeling that a very considerable part of the students who signed the paper were not so much interested in the formation of a university military organization as they were in securing for the University an Armory which could be used as a men's gymnasium—a result which, it was urged, would follow the organization of the University battalion," the Indiana *Alumni Quarterly* from April 1915 reported.

The students made the effort, but when all was said and done, it was unnecessary. On March 12, 1915, Shea made a motion that the next building erected on campus be a men's gymnasium. The motion was seconded by both Edwin Corr and the wonderfully named Ira Batman. The motion quickly passed 4–2 with James Fesler, Shea, Corr, and Batman voting for the new facility, and Rose and Robert Hamilton voting nay. The board ordered that President Bryan and a meeting made up of representatives of the faculty, students, alumni, "I" Men, and board of trustees be held at the university in the near future for the purpose of discussing the new gymnasium and all athletic affairs.

"The trustees realize the urgent need for a number of buildings," said the official report of the board of trustees from the meeting. "But, after full consideration, decided that on the whole it is best to begin with the erection of a Men's Gymnasium."

The fact that architect Robert Daggett was on hand with blueprints in hand seems to suggest that the result of the vote was a foregone conclusion, but no plan was accepted by the board at the time. It was expected that a site near the Dunn farmhouse at the east end of Seventh Street and north of Jordan Field would be used. It was a spot on a hill overlooking the eastern end of campus.

The announcement of the decision was made by none other than President Bryan himself, who spoke to a large crowd the next day at the Men's Gymnasium following a Bloomington-Fairmount game at the state high school tournament. Bryan's announcement was met with excitement, and the *Indiana Daily Student* reported, "The roof was fairly raised with the shouts of enthusiasm that went up when the President spoke the happy words."

The new gymnasium was expected to cost upward of $150,000, and it was reported that the work was expected to start that summer, with $66,000 from the university building fund helping to fund the early work.

John W. Cravens, a fascinating figure in his own right who managed to work his way up from undergraduate student at IU to become registrar, university secretary, and the secretary of the board of trustees, was ready to start to fill in the blanks a couple of days later.

"While no definite plans have been accepted," Cravens told the *Indiana Daily Student* March 16, 1915, "it is certain that the gymnasium will be the largest in Indiana and one of the largest in the West. It will doubtless be of stone. The new building will contain a gymnasium floor that will be one of the largest in the country and will also have an indoor field of large dimensions. By use of the indoor field, all forms of athletics can be carried on regardless of weather."

Cravens went on to admit that many high school gyms in the state of Indiana featured more floor space than IU's Men's Gymnasium, and he lamented the fact that ticket sales for the high school state basketball tournament had been limited to twelve hundred. The opening of the new building would allow crowds of up to at least twenty-five hundred people to attend games.

Cravens added that commencement exercises and other large events could be held at the building as well. He expected the foundation work to begin in the summer.

It didn't take long for various organizations to start to assert themselves while searching for a place to call their own. The "I" Men made it clear that they would like to have a special room that could be used as a lounging and club room for the "I" Men, and it could be used as a trophy room. IU, however, would depend on the reports of President Bryan, Daggett, athletes who had traveled to other venues, and other assorted committee members when it came to finalizing plans.

The Crimson finally would have their gymnasium and a fieldhouse to boot. It was just a matter of time.

The news of the impending Men's Gymnasium was met with plenty of excitement, but some of the buzz wore off over the summer. There was little news about the facility, although it seemed IU was going forward with the planning. Nobody in the student body seemed to know what was going on, and the gymnasium was starting to become a bit of a mystery.

Then a story appeared in the far-left column of the October 19, 1915, edition of the *Indiana Daily Student*: "HUGE DESTRUCTION SCHEME LEAKS OUT," the headline screamed. "Meager Details Known of Plot for Destruction of Life and Property."

The paper further reported that "two men have been seen acting suspiciously." Considering the turmoil in the world at that point, the story was bound to get plenty of attention.

It did.

"Meager details of a huge scheme involving the wholesale and violent destruction of life and property at Indiana University leaked out this morning from men prominent in the affairs of the University," the *Indiana Daily Student* said. "The names of the intended victims could not be learned. The time set for the attack is not definitely known, but it is thought to be within the week. Suspicion is directed toward two strangers seen recently about the campus, one of whom may be the bold burglar who operated successfully in Greek letter houses here last spring and summer. No arrests have been made."

The article went on to say that "some of the oldest servants of the University are threatened" and added that "a young man, tallying in some respects with the sorority thief, was observed on Jordan Field one afternoon last week industriously making pencil sketches upon a small white pad."

The next day, the *Indiana Daily Student* again worried about the rumors.

"Axe Still Hanging Over University," the October 20 edition said. "With the discovery of stores of tools and instruments of destruction on and about campus, and with the suspicion now directed toward two more Indiana University students, the situation created by the recent threats of violence to life and property at the State school has taken a new turn."

The tools found were said to be "long, slender and loaded or heavy at one end. This description is not unlike that of a certain type of infernal machine."

Cotton Berndt, the director of intramural athletics, was quoted as saying that he was confident the "secret agents" IU had working the case would not permit anything drastic to happen, but rumors flew that IU had set up a high-power searchlight to illuminate the dark corners of campus in case of an attack.

By October 21, the plotters were still missing, and the administration believed it was time to reveal all the facts they knew about the situation. A meeting was called at 7:30 p.m. at the Men's Gymnasium (the future Assembly Hall), and a statement was released saying, "We take this opportunity to give every man and woman connected with the University a chance to prepare for expected emergencies and to assist us wherever possible. All University people are requested to attend."

The meeting was called to quiet any hysteria as university officers and faculty members were bombarded with questions. Berndt stressed the importance of everyone attending the meeting, and he told the *Indiana Daily Student*, "An absence will be regarded as an indication of disloyalty. The meeting will be short. You better be there."

On a campus with an enrollment of fewer than nineteen hundred students, between six hundred and seven hundred people showed up at the gym for the meeting. The IU drum corps led a parade through campus to the gymnasium, and it was reported that many women were present. Seating for the ladies was reserved in the balcony, and as the appointed time arrived, Berndt walked to the front of the stage.

Let's allow the October 22 *Indiana Daily Student* tell the story of what happened next.

"Give 'em the axe, the axe, the axe; give 'em all the axe! The University authorities are no longer silent. But give what the axe? Why, 200 or more old apple trees standing on the site of the new Gymnasium. Yes; give 'em the axe tomorrow morning at 9 o'clock, every man and woman who wants to have a hand in clearing ground for the Indiana University's new Gymnasium; give 'em all the axe!"

The university had used the false rumors to drum up interest in an old-fashioned log rolling, and it worked to perfection. That's marketing, 1915 style.

Women weren't allowed to participate, save for the fact they would provide the "eats" by making sandwiches—with the food coming out of their own kitchens, it should be noted—and they would pass out apple cider as well. Every woman was expected to go to the parlor of the Student Building before 9:00 a.m. and to bring a nickel to offset the cost of the event.

Men, meanwhile, were asked to be prepared to work and to bring their own axes whenever possible. The Boosters Club had some axes on hand, but the club recognized that it would need more. A student named "Chic" Griffis closed the meeting with a yell session, and the always-nearby Albert Stump gave a speech that the *Indiana Daily Student* said appealed "to University people for such a united demonstration of loyalty tomorrow as has never before been known at Indiana." Stump went on to say that the ceremony would be one remembered for a lifetime.

When 9:00 a.m. rolled around on October 23, a sight that would be impossible—and legally irresponsible—these days developed. Men and women gathered around the Student Building, which is still wedged between Maxwell Hall and Owen Hall, and axes were handed out. Men were organized into teams, and with the IU band playing "Indiana" and cream-and-crimson streamers flying in the Indian summer air, hundreds of students began to parade through campus and toward the site of the new gymnasium.

As often happens when young men are involved, the parade slowly devolved into a race, and the next thing anybody knew, hundreds of students were running, jumping fences, and taking shortcuts—all with axes in hand, mind you—to see who would be the first to start in on an apple tree. Somehow everyone survived without chopping off an appendage before the logging commenced. Luella Smith, president of the Women's League, quickly set up shop on the grounds, and white-aproned coeds passed out food. The *Indiana Daily Student* turned to the flowery prose of the time to describe the beverages.

"While trees crashed down on every side, the old hand-power cider mill creaked out its stream of Winesap liquid to quench the thirst of the Gymnasium pioneers."

Bringing down the trees proved to be hard work, and the draw of food, cider, and the ladies convinced more than one of the men to take repeated breaks. Older men and women from Bloomington helped out some, but the *Indiana Daily Student* said they left the heavy work to the young folks.

President Bryan was involved in felling the trees, and he was one of approximately five hundred men to take part in the effort. Another two hundred women were on hand, and the trees fell quickly, but not everything went smoothly. The handle of the cistern pump at the Dunn house, which stood on the property, had been removed, and the Boosters Club was forced to run and get water from the university. Superintendent Eugene Kerr later managed to roll two barrels of water to the scene.

Problems with the cider mill, meanwhile, cropped up when the owner of the mill, for some unknown reason, removed its handle. The men tried to work the mill anyway but with little success.

"After a few rounds they came to the conclusion that it is about as hard to get cider out of a crankless cider mill as it is to get blood out of a turnip," the *Indiana Daily Student* reported. "The cider fiends quit and went to sawing wood."

It took only an hour for the western half of the orchard to be brought down, and when the dust settled, the brush made huge piles on the site. Everyone had the same idea about what to do with all the logs, leaves, twigs, and sticks. Once that wood dried, the Indiana faithful were going to have the biggest bonfire IU had ever seen.

While the trees fell, Indiana's administration was busy with the business of building the Men's Gymnasium. Invitations for bids had been sent out the previous day by Cravens, who outlined the strict rules for outfits looking to land the contracts. The plans for the new Men's Gymnasium were specific and impressive. Daggett had a clear vision for what he wanted to build.

> The proposed Gymnasium for Indiana University is to be built in the Collegiate Gothic style, or more properly speaking, Tudor Gothic. The building is to be approximately 240 ft. by 328 ft. facing west, and forming the head or west end of the athletic field. There are two main entrances to the building from the west, leading into wide corridors at the end of which are stairs giving access to basement and second floor, these corridors also lead to the large indoor field at the back of the Gymnasium building proper.

On the first or ground floor are located the Swimming Pool, Team Rooms for Varsity and Freshmen, Main Locker Room and the Toilets, Showers, Drying Rooms, etc. On the second floor are located the Gymnasium, Lounging Room and Offices of the Physical Director, Athletic Director, Medical Director and Coaches. In the basement are located the Hand Ball Courts, bowling alleys and heating and ventilating apparatus. The main gymnasium is to be 90′ wide by 160′ long, well lighted and ventilated and occupying the central portion of the building. This room is to be open to the roof, which is supported by steel trusses. The walls of the Gymnasium are to be of a light bluff [sic] colored brick.

To the north of the Gymnasium and separated from it by the stairway and Hall is the Lounging Room, 28′ wide by 82′ long. This room is to be finished with a paneled oak wainscoting and beamed ceiling, with a large fireplace at one end. To the south of the Gymnasium room and separated from it by the stairway and hall are the general offices. Above the stairway and hall at each end of the Gymnasium is to be a balcony, overlooking the Gymnasium. In cases of basket-ball games, etc., bleacher seats can be arranged around Gymnasium seating approximately 2,500 people. The swimming pool and locker room are underneath the gymnasium on the first floor.

The swimming pool room is 52 feet by 114 feet with a pool 30 feet by 90 feet and seats for approximately 200 spectators. This room and the pool are to be lined with tile. Separating the pool room from the main locker room is the shower bath room, containing 22 showers. The main locker room has ample capacity for 1,000 lockers and has direct connection with the indoor field and with the gymnasium above. Every effort possible has been made to make the lockers and locker rooms sanitary and sterilizing apparatus and drying apparatus have been provided for the clothing. The varsity and freshman team rooms are at either end of the building with separate entrances to the athletic field and with separate steam, shower and toilet rooms. The Faculty locker room on this floor also has its separate toilet and shower rooms.

The indoor field is 150 feet by 200 feet dirt floor with a running track having 12 laps to a mile. This large space is to be spanned with steel trusses and well lighted from above. At the east end of the indoor field a large stage has been provided, large enough and arranged so that any kind of production can be given, and by placing seats in the indoor field, large audiences can be accommodated.

The building is to be fireproof. The heating, ventilating and lighting is to be of the best, and the building furnished and equipped complete according to the latest and best methods.

When all was said and done, IU received a total of nineteen bids for the general contract. Indiana decided to go with a familiar contractor: A. E. Kemmer of Lafayette, Indiana, was awarded the deal, partially thanks to the work he had done on improvements to Owen Hall in 1914. Although his bid was higher than expected—in fact, all the bids were much higher than IU had expected—Kemmer's bid was some $40,000 lower than his closest competitor. As tough a pill as it may be to swallow, the fact is the Men's Gymnasium was built by a Purdue grad.

Other contracts for heating, plumbing, excavation, and electrical work would eventually add more than $60,000 to that total, and the final number didn't include a major portion of the construction. During the board of trustees meeting to accept the bid, Shea entered a motion that the construction of an indoor field and a stage for events be postponed. It seems the cost of such construction was much higher than expected, and Indiana simply couldn't justify the cost at that time. A future fieldhouse could be added, but for the time being, just the gymnasium would have to do.

All that was left was to actually get the shovels in the ground. Or, in IU's case, a plow.

Indiana was nothing if not creative when it came to getting students involved on campus in 1915. Six weeks after tapping the student body to do the dirty work of clearing the grounds, IU turned to the students yet again when it came to turning the soil. On December 7, President Bryan found himself standing behind a plow with a rope reported to be at least two hundred feet long attached to it. The Boosters Club split the men into teams, each with its own captain, with two aims. First, it was the captain's responsibility to get the members of his team to stop at the same time once the plow had been moved. Second, the captains were responsible for making sure the members of their teams didn't get too worked up and try to steal the plow (because really, who wouldn't want his own plow?).

Arrangements were made to have a photographer on hand, and participants who signed up would get the opportunity to own a piece of the rope used to move the plow once they were finished. The Boosters Club would cut up the rope and send it to the students in the future.

Before the groundbreaking could get underway, President Bryan made a short speech, which was reported verbatim in the December 8 *Indiana Daily Student* just above a notice that Jordan Field would be flooded to create an ice-skating rink: "The gymnasium is a symbol of the University's creed. It stands for health—that is, for the whole man. An athlete who has neglected his intellect and is not fitted to take part in this age of intelligence is not a whole man. A student who has trained his intellect and neglected his body is not a whole man. He is not ready for the battle. The University stands for the whole man, and this great gymnasium is one part of the means of securing that end."

Alumni secretary Ralph Sollitt made some short comments, and Albert Stump—naturally—was on hand to give the students' point of view. Then, as the IU band played and some thousand spectators looked on, Bursar U. H. Smith gave the order to the couple of hundred men on the ropes, and at 4:15 p.m., the plow started to move through the soft ground.

It was at roughly twenty feet that the rope snapped, and just about all two hundred men tumbled onto that soft ground.

Still, the day was a huge success, and Kemmer's contractors jumped right into the work of excavating and getting the facility off the ground. After all, with a deadline of January 1, 1917, in place, there was a lot of work to be done over the next thirteen months.

The bane of builders in Bloomington, then as now, is the limestone that serves as bedrock for most of the area. Unfortunately for the workers, an unusual amount of rock was found under the construction site, and it took weeks of blasting to properly excavate. In early January, Kerr reported to the *Indiana Daily Student* that it would be at least sixty days to finish the work of excavation of the whole site, but in the meantime, concrete could be poured in portions of the construction to build a foundation.

Work progressed relatively smoothly through the spring and summer, with Kemmer using the old Dunn house as construction headquarters. Indiana limestone from Bloomington's own John W. Hoadley Company was used, and the G. C. Davis Hardware Co., another Bloomington business, provided the tin work. As the facility rose out of the ground, the brickwork on the east side of the gymnasium provided a glimpse of the future.

Rough limestone was used for most of the building, but a triangle-shaped area of buffed brick took up a large portion of the east side, showing the general outline of where a future fieldhouse would go. When the fieldhouse was eventually added a decade later, the brick was incorporated into the design, and the contrast between the buff brick and the rough stone can still be seen in the upper portion of the Bill Garrett Fieldhouse, where the two buildings meet.

Excitement grew as work progressed. The stonework was completed in late August or early September of 1916, and the trusses that would span the width of the building were put in place. The trusses were 92.8 feet in length and weighed six tons each. The trusses were lifted to the main floor in sections and were then riveted and bolted together. Then they were lifted in one piece and hoisted into place. Each truss took two days to prepare.

Meanwhile, at least two train cars of black slate roofing tile were required once the trusses were put in place, and some two miles of pipe were laid at the facility, including five thousand feet of cast-iron soil pipe and five thousand feet of galvanized iron supply pipe. Each of the fifty-one showerheads in the facility included nonscalding valves to regulate the heating of water.

Finally, some $17,000 in marble tile was used in the pool area and in hallways. The designs of the tiles ranged from lions to crabs to flowers to crosses, among other things, and they included what would become an extremely unfortunate design down the road.

Swastikas.

The swastika tiles have turned as many heads as the coeds at the Men's Gymnasium since the rise of Adolf Hitler's Nazi Party, but when they were laid in 1916, the Nazi Party had not been founded, and the swastika was seen as a symbol of health, life, and good luck. During World War I, the American Forty-Fifth Division wore swastika patches, and swastika postcards were seen as a friendly greeting.

Despite the connotations, the IU administration resisted changing the tiles at the Men's Gymnasium over the years. In 1994, however, IU's Racial Incidents Team, responding to complaints, put up a plaque explaining the history of the tiles.

"Members of the campus community have taken exception to some of these tiles which are shaped like swastikas," the plaque explains. "This wing of the HPER [Health, Physical Education, and Recreation] building was built in 1917, before the Nazi party popularly adopted the swastika as its national symbol of world domination. Only with the Nazi rise of power was the meaning of the swastika associated with abusive power and horrible domination.

These tiles are not intended to be associated with such meanings. They were placed here with the original intent of wishing health and prosperity to all. Thank you for your understanding and cooperation."

The tiles were finally removed by the university in the summer of 2019.

The December 15, 1916, *Indiana Daily Student* finally announced that Foundation Day, January 19, 1917, would serve as the official dedication day for the Men's Gymnasium. The Athletic Association also announced that "the gymnasium was not to be used for any other purpose but gymnastics and athletic contests. No exceptions will be made for social affairs or lectures."

That rule wouldn't last long, but we'll get to that in a minute.

New Year's Day of 1917 came and went without the Men's Gymnasium being a finished product, and Kemmer explained that several shipments of materials had not yet arrived. The basketball floor, however, had arrived and been installed, and it was a unique structure. Besides being the normal hardwood basketball floor that was (and still is) the standard, the Men's Gymnasium featured banks in each corner of the floor outside of the sidelines and baselines that would allow joggers in the facility to turn corners without slowing down. The basketball court also included another unique feature: glass backboards.

The backboards weren't entirely glass. The rim was mounted on a piece of wood at the bottom of the backboard, but the rest of the backboard was a slab of glass made by the Nurre Mirror Plate Company of Bloomington. The one-and-a-half-inch-thick glass allowed fans to see the game unobstructed.

The IU basketball team took the floor for its first practice January 8, and the January 8 *Indiana Daily Student* reported that the glass backboards "puzzled" the basketball players. It also was reported that the "immensity of the floor soon winded the men also, but nevertheless they were given a strenuous workout." A number of students stopped by to check out the facility, and it didn't take long for an unseemly element to make an appearance.

Despite the presence of lockers fourteen inches square and thirty-six inches high that were supposedly safe for valuables, some freshmen were given temporary lockers that didn't actually have any locks on them. As the freshmen worked out in the gymnasium on the second floor, thieves made their way into the locker room and took off with ten dollars in cash and three watches. Interestingly, the watches were actually recovered by the Bloomington police in early March. The ten dollars were never found.

The Men's Gymnasium was, indeed, ready for Indiana's battle with Iowa on January 19. A procession was to begin at 9:15 a.m. for Foundation Day ceremonies, and the gymnasium was decked out in the colors of Argentina—in honor of Ambassador Romulo S. Naon, who was on hand—and the United States. That night, the glass backboards seemed to confuse all the players. Indiana won its first game on its home court by a count of 12–7 in what was described in the *Indiana Daily Student* as a "fast, hard-fought" contest. IU suffered its first loss at the new facility January 28 when Purdue took home a 22–15 victory, and the Crimson closed out their first year at the Men's Gymnasium with a 3–3 record.

The project was fully approved, and Indiana took possession of the facility late that winter. The final cost of the facility was $220,488.08, with Kemmer going less than $1,000 over his budget. In July of that year, the west side of the Men's Gymnasium was scheduled to undergo landscaping work. The hill in front of the gym was shaped into three terraces, a feature that exists to this day. Concrete walks were laid to allow students and fans to come and go without walking across the grass.

The opening of the Men's Gymnasium led to an explosion of athletics at Indiana. The existence of a quality swimming facility triggered the founding of the IU swim team, and the school formed a boxing team as well. The construction also prompted the creation of a six-hole golf course north of the gymnasium. A course design expert was brought in from Chicago, and thanks to the hard work of the landscaping team, the course was ready for play by 1917. Unfortunately, the links wouldn't stick around long. In the mid-1920s, the links were closed, and the land was used for the construction of Memorial Stadium.

The Men's Gymnasium was actually supposed to trigger a major expansion of the sports facilities. Some contemporary drawings show Memorial Stadium being planned directly east of the gymnasium through what is now the Eskenazi Museum of Art and toward the IU Auditorium. Tennis courts were initially planned, and a home for the university president was planned as well. The president's house was the only construction that became a reality in the long run.

Intramural sports took a huge step forward thanks to the gymnasium, and the track and baseball teams had much more space to work out in inclement weather. When the United States finally entered World War I in March, just a few months after the opening of the gymnasium, the basement of the building was used as a rifle range. It would continue its use as the home of the IU rifle team well into the second half of the century.

The Men's Gymnasium was used as a barracks during World War I, and the facility helped keep IU students in top shape for military duty. Once the war ended, and enrollment exploded, the Men's Gymnasium allowed the school to handle the influx of students. The rule about the facility being used only for athletic events was pushed out of the way as well. Multiple dances were held there, including one massive party following Indiana's shocking 12–6 win over Syracuse on November 22, 1919. The alumni and students "went wild," according to the 1920 *Arbutus*, and some eight hundred people crowded into the gymnasium for the annual "Blanket Hop" of Sigma Delta Chi. A total of twelve "I" blankets were purchased with the proceeds from the dance.

The 1921 junior prom was a fancy evening at the Men's Gymnasium, with students enjoying dancing in the gym, and card tables were set up in both the study lounge and the pool area. The ceiling of the pool area was decorated with streamers, and a small suspension bridge was built to go across the pool and give young lovers a chance to walk over the water.

The growing popularity of basketball saw the gym packed for just about every game, and the Indiana high school basketball tournament returned for a few years. Indiana's first All-American, Everett Dean, played in the Men's Gymnasium, and he returned as head coach for the 1924–25 season. Dean quickly built a successful program, and by the middle of the 1920s, the old plans for a fieldhouse were revived, thanks in large part to the growing popularity of IU's team. Construction began outside the Men's Gymnasium, and the fieldhouse included plans for a drastically expanded basketball facility, relegating the Men's Gymnasium to little more than a backup court for basketball. Three days after the Ritz Theatre, which would eventually become the Von Lee on Kirkwood Avenue, opened, the Crimson played their final game at the facility, scoring a 36–34 win over Michigan en route to a 15–2 record and a Big Ten championship. IU held its final practice on the Men's Gymnasium floor on December 5, 1928, before christening the fieldhouse three days later. The Crimson men's basketball team finished their time at the Men's Gymnasium with an 86–31 record.

Basketball may have been finished at the Men's Gymnasium, but varsity sports were far from over at the facility. Swimming used the pool at the facility until the Royer Pool was opened in 1962, and sports such as fencing, volleyball, and gymnastics continued to use the facility. An addition to the north end of the building was made in the early 1960s when the School of Health, Physical Education, and Recreation (HPER) greatly expanded the facility, which allowed the HPER to bring all of its departments under one roof.

The construction of the new Assembly Hall in the early 1970s signaled the end of varsity sports at the Men's Gymnasium save for rare occasions. Volleyball and gymnastics moved out during this time, and the Men's Gymnasium has been the home of the HPER for thousands of students over the past forty-plus years.

The Men's Gymnasium is one of the monuments to the history of Indiana athletics. It has watched the campus rise around it, and it towered over Jordan Field until that facility was paved over during the late 1950s.

It also served as the catalyst for some much-needed stability in IU athletics by providing a forward-thinking venue that finally helped IU catch up with some of its rivals.

FIGURE 6.1. The Dunn family home stood at the top of a hill in Dunn Meadow overlooking an apple orchard. The home, shown here in 1900, stood on the spot where the new Men's Gymnasium would be built in 1917. *IU Archives P0034821*

FIGURE 6.2. IU president William Lowe Bryan and his wife, Charlotte, pose after bringing down trees in the Dunn apple orchard. *IU Archives P0020482*

FIGURE 6.3. The new Men's Gymnasium as it looked when it opened in 1917. *IU Archives P0026071*

7

A God in Bloomington

Clarence Childs had a problem.

His first year as the IU's head football coach couldn't exactly be considered a success. After being hired in early 1914 to take over the lagging IU football program, Childs hadn't ignited the gridiron passions in Bloomington. Worse yet, he didn't even lead his team to improvement on the field. The 1913 squad went 3–4, including a 2–4 record in the Big Nine Conference under former head coach James Sheldon. Childs's 1914 squad could muster no more than the same 3–4 record overall, and the team went just 1–4 in league play. Wins over DePauw, Northwestern, and Miami (Ohio) weren't exactly going to cut it, at least not in Childs's eyes.

Then again, failure was never really part of the equation for Childs. The Wooster, Ohio, native turned hard work in the classroom into a spot in the Yale School of Law in the first decade of the twentieth century, and he found time to excel on the field as well. He played tackle for the football team during the fall, he wrestled in the winter, and he was a track and field athlete in the spring. He was known for having a tough work ethic and a soft heart—traits he openly displayed.

For instance, when he was a senior in the Yale School of Law, he served as a witness in a trial that saw a man named Arthur Jacobs sent to prison for eight months on a theft conviction. Jacobs's wife began sobbing at the verdict, and it so moved Childs that he took up a collection for the woman. He first collected thirty-five dollars from the crowd in the courtroom to help the woman, and then he and eighteen other Yale students donated their witness fees, swelling the total donation to forty-six dollars.

On top of taking the lead in the courtroom, Childs was also a leader for the Yale track team, where he was named captain of the squad for the 1911 season. By January 1912, Childs had resigned his position as captain to focus on finishing school, and he also planned to put all his efforts into the hammer throw. He had a knack for the event, and when the 1912 Olympic trials rolled around, Childs earned a spot on the US track and field team that would travel to Stockholm, Sweden.

Childs didn't just enjoy the Olympic experience, either. He made it count. He earned a bronze medal with a toss of 48.17 meters (a little more than 158 feet), missing a silver medal by roughly nine inches.

When Childs returned to the United States, he landed at Wooster University, where he served as director of athletics. He served in that capacity until IU came calling in February 1914, and he took over as Crimson football coach in September 1914 (oh, and he was the track and field coach at IU, too).

With all that success under his belt, Childs couldn't stand pat and simply accept Indiana's struggles on Jordan Field, which was the home of the football, baseball, and track and field squads. He knew he had to do something big, something that could create a buzz around the football program and inject some life into a sport that hadn't seen a winning season since 1910. Something simply had to be done, and Childs had a big idea for IU.

He would get by with a little help from his friends. Actually, just one friend.

One of the overlooked aspects of the Olympics is the ability to network. The greatest athletes from all over the world gather, and it gives those athletes a chance to meet and get to know one another. During the 1912 Stockholm Olympics, athletes had more than two months to get acquainted (the games of the V Olympiad opened May 5 and closed July 22), and Childs took the opportunity to get to know the biggest star of the games.

James Francis "Jim" Thorpe was born in Prague, Oklahoma, in 1887, and if you don't know who he is, prepare to be amazed. Thorpe was born to mixed-race parents—his father was of Irish and Sac and Fox Indian descent, and his mother had French and Potawatomi Indian ancestry—which meant Thorpe would be considered by the society of the time to be of Native

American descent, greatly limiting his opportunities. He enrolled in Carlisle Industrial Indian School in Pennsylvania in 1904, and his athletic career began in 1907 when he joined the track and field squad. Other sports quickly followed, and he eventually competed in football, baseball, lacrosse, and ballroom dancing (yes, ballroom dancing).

Thorpe was Carlisle's best track and field athlete, and his coach, Glenn "Pop" Warner, wasn't wild about the idea of Thorpe playing such a physical game as football. But Thorpe insisted he be given a tryout, and Warner finally relented. Legend has it that Thorpe ran through and past the defense not once but twice on the same play, turning back to attack the defense again before running over to Warner, flipping the future legend the ball and saying, "Nobody is going to tackle Jim."

From that point on, the six-foot-one, 190-pound Thorpe was destined to be a star on the gridiron. He was named first-team All-American in 1911 and 1912. As a running back, defensive back, kicker, and punter, Thorpe scored all of Carlisle's points in an 18–15 upset of Harvard in 1911; and in a 27–6 win over Army in 1912, Thorpe again caught the attention of the nation when he scored on a ninety-two-yard touchdown run that was called back on a penalty. On the next play, he scored on a ninety-seven-yard run. During that game, by the way, Thorpe ran over an Army linebacker who tried to tackle him, injuring the cadet in the process. The linebacker, a sophomore named Dwight D. Eisenhower, was never physically the same after that, and he later quit football to concentrate on his military career. Eventually, Eisenhower went into politics, where he did pretty well for himself.

But Thorpe's biggest splash came when he went out for the US track and field team for the 1912 Olympics. He earned a spot on the squad in four different events—the pentathlon, the decathlon, the high jump, and the long jump—and he trained on the ship ride from the United States to Sweden. Thorpe first competed in the pentathlon, an event that features athletes competing in five different events. He took first place in the broad jump, the 220-yard dash, the mile run, and the high jump, and he finished third in the javelin. That same day, he finished fourth in the high jump standalone event, and he placed seventh in the long jump.

His final event was the decathlon, a grueling ten-part test that, in 1912, asked Thorpe to compete in the following disciplines: broad jump, shot put, pole vault, hundred-yard sprint, hammer throw, discus, mile run, high jump, high hurdles, and javelin. Despite his heavy workload heading into the decathlon, Thorpe crushed the competition, taking home first place in the shot put, the high jump, the 110-meter hurdles, and the mile run. He finished in the top four in all ten events, earning 8,413 points, an Olympic record that would stand for nearly two decades.

When Thorpe was awarded his gold medals on the final day of the Olympics, King Gustav V of Sweden presented Thorpe with his medal and various awards. After awarding Thorpe his prize, King Gustav grabbed Thorpe's arm and said, "You, sir, are the greatest athlete in the world." Thorpe simply answered, "Thanks, King."

When Thorpe returned home, he was honored with a ticker-tape parade down Broadway in New York, and he discovered he was the most famous athlete in America. After finishing his football career at Carlisle, Thorpe suffered a major setback when newspapers began reporting that during the summers of 1909 and 1910, Thorpe had played minor league baseball in the East Carolina League, earning between two and thirty-five dollars a week. Unlike a number of other collegiate players at the time, Thorpe used his real name, making it easy for reporters to track down the information.

In other words, it turned out Thorpe was a professional athlete at the time of the 1912 Olympics, and under the strict amateur rules at the time, he should not have been eligible to compete for the United States in Stockholm. The Amateur Athletic Union, which then put together the Olympic team, withdrew Thorpe's status as an amateur athlete retroactively, and the International Olympic Committee (IOC) stripped Thorpe of his medals.

On the bright side, with his professional status no longer a secret, Thorpe was officially a free agent in the sports world. Eventually he settled on baseball, the most popular sport in the country, as his chosen profession. He signed with the New York Giants late in the 1913 season, and he was part of a worldwide barnstorming tour with the Giants and Chicago White Sox. During the trip, Thorpe met Pope Pius X, Abbas II Hilmi Bey of Egypt, and Britain's King George V, and he reportedly wrestled with another baseball player on the floor of the Colosseum in Rome.

As a member of the Giants, Thorpe was largely a showpiece, and he didn't actually get much playing time. He was used as an attraction as his name carried so much weight, but he rarely got into games. He appeared in a total of sixty-six games for the Giants from 1913 to 1915, and by the summer of 1915,

Thorpe was looking for a change. Baseball didn't seem to be working out, and he was ready for a new challenge.

Fortunately for Childs, he was looking for change as well.

No one is quite sure exactly when Childs contacted Thorpe about the possibility of his former Olympic teammate joining him as backfield coach with the Crimson. For the season, Thorpe would be paid a sum of $1,000 plus a room for his family at a Bloomington hotel. By early September, Thorpe had agreed to come to Bloomington.

"Jim Thorpe to Coach Indiana," the September 2, 1915, the *Indianapolis Star* trumpeted. Subheads screamed, "World's Greatest Athlete Will Help Childs with Backfield Men" and "Noted Indian Will Start Work When Baseball Season Is Ended." The *Star* wrote:

> This news, coming as it does on the eve of the opening of the season, should serve to act as a tonic to athletics at the Bloomington institution. That Thorpe should be—and no doubt will be—of great assistance to Coach Childs in developing a powerful football eleven at Indiana this year cannot well be gainsaid. Coach Childs said last night over the long-distance telephone that he proposes to turn over the back field men to Thorpe and devote most of his own time to the linesmen. Thorpe probably will be unable to join Coach Childs' staff until the close of the National League baseball season, for he is now playing with the New York Giants. The season will close in early October, and Thorpe has advised Mr. Childs that he immediately will come on to Bloomington.

By late September, Childs was putting his players through their paces on a very soggy Jordan Field, a place famous for its inability to shed water. With the days growing shorter, Childs had to move practice to the track oval at Jordan Field, which recently had been fitted with temporary high-power electric lights. Childs had to be itching for Thorpe to arrive because one of his assistants, Dan Goodman, had left the team to "assume new duties with the Ford Motor Company in Indianapolis."

The *Indiana Daily Student* finally announced Thorpe's hiring locally in its September 28 edition.

> James J. Thorpe, the famous Carlisle Indian athlete, reputed the world's greatest athlete, will arrive here in a few days to assist Coach Childs in football. He is at present with the New York Giants, having signed a contract

to play baseball with them two years ago. Big league baseball will close October 8, but it is thought that he will be able to leave a few days before the close of the season.

Thorpe will take charge of the backfield upon his arrival and will, no doubt, be able to turn out a strong offensive from the fine material on hand. ... As Coach Childs has a large squad of nearly forty men, Thorpe will be of great assistance.

It's time to take a step back and recognize the shockwave the announcement of Thorpe's hiring sent through the Bloomington community. Simply put, no real comparison can be made with any modern athlete. The closest might be Bo Jackson, who was a Heisman Trophy winner and NFL star while also becoming an All-Star baseball player. To match Thorpe, Bo would also have needed to win the Tour de France or an Olympic Gold medal. Then, Jackson would have had to have come to IU to serve as an assistant coach during the prime of his career. A better comparison might be if Michael Jordan had continued to play basketball throughout the 1990s while also becoming a major league baseball player and winning the one-hundred-meter sprint at the Olympics. It's mind-boggling. The fact that Thorpe would be coming to little ol' Indiana University to help the foundering football team was staggering. Thorpe, however, wouldn't arrive in time to help the Crimson for their season opener against DePauw. Still, as the campus buzzed over the unveiling of plans for a new gymnasium to be built north of Jordan Field, Childs and his IU squad got off to a fast start to the season, beating DePauw 7–0. A player identified only as McIntosh scored the only touchdown of the game in the second quarter.

A few days after the DePauw game, the *Indiana Daily Student* announced that Thorpe would be arriving in Bloomington on Thursday, October 7:

After some three weeks of anxious waiting, McGraw's national past-timers (John McGraw coached the Giants at the time) turn over to the University coaching staff one of the greatest athletes the world has ever known, James Thorpe. He and his family will arrive in this city Thursday evening at 7 o'clock. Thorpe will take up his duties as assistant coach Friday afternoon.

Students, alumni, and, in fact, the entire college world looks forward to the coming of this great athlete, with great eagerness to know exactly how his coaching will compare with his known ability as a player. In fact, the thing foremost in the minds of these men is, can this All-American star teach the Indiana backfield men the tricks that made him so famous at Carlisle? Coach Childs and Thorpe, assisted by old stars such as Coval, Rab Hare, Dick Miller, George Cook and Howard Paddock, working on some forty-five huskies, should round in shape a team such as never before wore Cream and Crimson uniforms. If the old injury jinx will stay away and let out of his hospital those already convicted, Indiana will have no one to feel afraid of.

Thorpe finally arrived, and he made his first appearance at Jordan Field the next day. The IU faithful showed up in droves for practice, first gathering at 4:00 p.m. outside the Student Building before marching through campus to Jordan Field. Chic Griffis, the yell leader for the Crimson (a precursor to cheerleaders), taught the assembled crowd new cheers for the upcoming game against Miami (Ohio), and he also called for "nine cheers for Thorpe" and "nine cheers for Childs" as the Crimson practiced. A number of alumni made their way into town as well to get a glimpse of the superstar on the Crimson staff.

Thorpe may have fired up the crowd, but he couldn't have had much of an immediate impact on the Crimson. Still, IU hammered Miami (Ohio) 41–0 in front of a huge crowd at Jordan Field October 9, jumping out to a 34–0 lead by halftime. The *Indiana Daily Student* didn't report on Thorpe's movements during the game—he wasn't mentioned, although it was mentioned in the paper that Bertha Whitaker, class of 1919, had visited her parents in Martinsville that Sunday—but the fans thrilled to the sight of Thorpe on the sideline.

By the next Tuesday, Thorpe was finally getting in some real work with the kickers. He worked with two players named Clair Scott and Frank Whitaker prior to a scrimmage, and he apparently made an impression.

"Before the scrimmage, assistant coach Thorpe had the kickers out in the center of the arena instructing them in getting off their punts in good form," the *Indiana Daily Student* wrote. "The Indian's long, twisting spirals were not duplicated by either Scott or Whitaker, although both Crimson backs showed much improvement over past performances."

A few days later, Thorpe wowed observers again. He worked with the kickers before the team left for its battle with the University of Chicago in the Windy City, and Thorpe put on a show in practice.

"In showing the kickers how to boot the ball, the Indian sent the pigskin seventy and seventy-five yards on an average and was roundly applauded," the October 15, 1915, *Indiana Daily Student* reported. "Halfbacks Scott and Gray, who do the punting for Indiana, made several good punts of forty-five and fifty yards. Thorpe then instructed Whitaker and [Earl] Peckinpaugh in the art of place-kicking. [Archie] Erehart also loosened up and sent some drop-kicks between the goal posts from the thirty-five and 40-yard lines. Thorpe left last evening with the ten men in the kicking department for Chicago, where they will try out on Stagg Field today."

The Crimson trip to Chicago to take on Amos Alonzo Stagg's Maroons put a chip on IU's shoulders. Chicago had embarrassed Indiana 34–0 a year earlier, and the Crimson were ready for some revenge. With Jim Thorpe in their back pocket, Indiana couldn't go wrong.

At least that was the thought in Bloomington. Unfortunately for IU fans, the story was one that would become familiar over the years. Poor tackling, poor line play, and penalties led to a 13–7 loss to the Maroons, much to the chagrin of the five hundred IU fans in attendance and the three hundred more hanging out at the Union to read the results as they were sent down from Chicago. On the bright side, the students in Bloomington could chew away their sorrows by gnawing on two barrels of apples that were donated by the Union.

The Chicago media hyped Thorpe's appearance in the city and almost completely overlooked the fact that Childs, not Thorpe, was IU's head coach. More than one paper described the game by mentioning "Indian Jim Thorpe's Hoosier footballers," and Thorpe far overshadowed the IU football team. Meanwhile, back in Bloomington, the *Indiana Daily Student* tackled the story of Thorpe's wife, Iva, who was settling into her new home. As part of the weekly "Fair Sex Forum" in the newspaper, Iva, who was just identified as "Mrs. Thorpe," was repeatedly asked about her Native American ancestry, but she disappointed readers by maintaining that she couldn't lend any insight into what goes on at an Indian reservation.

"As I told you before, I'm only one-sixteenth Indian," Iva told the *Indiana Daily Student*. "No, I never lived on a reservation. I haven't a single 'blanket Indian' relative that I know of, but Mr. Thorpe has. Oh, no! I never wore a blanket."

Iva did take the time to brag about her five-month-old son. Sadly, Jim Jr. would pass away at the age of two in 1917.

After returning to Bloomington following the game, Thorpe spent some time on Jordan Field practicing kicking by himself with few witnesses around. An *Indiana Daily Student* reporter, however, was there to capture the moment for posterity in the October 19 edition:

> A little exhibition of drop-kicking was given yesterday afternoon, unknown to the regular bleacherites. No one was around—there was no grandstand play—just a step, a quick swing of the leg and a double-thud as the ball hit ground and cleated shoe at the same instant. The kicker was "Jim" Thorpe, late addition to the Crimson coaching staff. He stood on the line which divides the gridiron into two equal portions, a little toward the sideline to avoid the mud. There was a flash of red and brown as his leg swung to meet the rising pigskin and away sailed the ball, end over end, squarely between the white posts at the end of the field.
>
> The long kick was accomplished with so much ease and grace that it appeared the least difficult feat in the world, but the big Indian merely smiled. It's not "being done" on many gridirons this season, however, so old Jordan Field ought to feel mighty proud.

In other words, Thorpe quietly walked out to the unmanicured field and started pounding fifty-yard dropkicks through the goal posts. Let's see LeBron James do that.

With a bye week on the schedule following the Chicago game, the coaching staff focused on the fundamentals during practice. Thorpe worked with his players, and great lengths were taken to try to shield Jordan Field from spies. Barbed wire was placed along the top of the wooden fence that surrounded the field, and guards were posted to shoo off anybody who wanted to take a peek through knotholes. The Crimson suffered a setback when assistant coach F. E. Ferguson, who was working with the offensive line, broke a bone in his foot during practice. That injury had to get the attention of Thorpe, who was still interested in playing professional sports.

It's also likely that Thorpe could have taken some part in the event held just north of Jordan Field October 23, which saw hundreds of IU students take part in clearing the area where the new Men's Gymnasium would be built. The groundbreaking saw axes handed out, and for more than two hours, male students chopped down an apple orchard that occupied the site. Coeds handed out cider and sandwiches, and a good time was had by all.

Considering there wasn't much to do in Bloomington, and the groundbreaking was the biggest event in town on a Saturday afternoon in October, it's reasonable to imagine that Thorpe made an appearance.

Indiana's trip to Indy to take on Washington and Lee on October 30 was a huge event in and of itself, and the game was sold out. It was estimated that three-quarters of the student body at IU—including the girls!—would be attending the game. Special trains were scheduled, and Indiana governor Samuel M. Ralston would be in attendance.

For his part, Thorpe had been developing new talent on the kicking corps. Russell Hathaway, a nineteen-year-old fullback, had recently joined the group and was already kicking forty-yard field goals thanks to Thorpe's instruction. In all, six different Crimson were showing promise as kickers, with at least five players ripping punts of fifty or sixty yards in practice, and Erehart was kicking field goals from all kinds of angles from twenty-five, thirty, and forty yards out.

Despite all the work, IU's kickers missed when it mattered most. Twice in the third quarter, Erehart missed dropkicks, one from at least forty yards out. Those misses played a key role in IU's 7–7 tie with Washington and Lee, and the largest crowd ever to see a game in Indianapolis to that point—eighty-five hundred—was at least treated to a close game.

The game may have been a toss-up on the field, but IU was a huge winner at the box office. Thanks at least partly to the presence of Thorpe in the big city, IU cleared between $5,000 and $6,000 in the game, a staggering amount for the time.

Another big payday would undoubtedly come when Indiana traveled to Ohio State on November 6, and Thorpe spent his week working with the Crimson on their punting, drop-kicking, and punt coverage. Thorpe also got involved in teaching IU how to tackle, and there was quite a bit of excitement surrounding the idea that with Thorpe teaching the team his secrets, the Buckeyes literally wouldn't know what hit them.

Unfortunately for IU, Ohio State was Ohio State even then. The Crimson were flagged for more than one hundred yards in penalties, and the Buckeyes won 10–9. Thorpe's work with the kickers didn't pay off as IU missed five field-goal attempts, with Erehart kicking one along the ground over the goal line and another from IU's Harry Gray getting blocked.

Childs was livid with his players, and he drove his players hard in practice during the next week. IU's coach led his linemen in drills to improve their blocking on kicks, and he worked with the line on techniques to block kicks. Thorpe, meanwhile, worked with every single member of the backfield to try to find a consistent kicker. A total of eighteen players attempted kicks in practice, and Reagle Acre, a class of 1917 student from Sigma Delta Psi, joined the team after going six of eight from forty yards in a tryout.

The *Indiana Daily Student* hoped the work would make an impact.

"Childs, assisted by Thorpe, is working hard to develop a steady toe and a line that will hold like so much stone," the November 9 edition reported. "If this can be accomplished, Northwestern and Purdue will have to use flying machines to win."

Indiana didn't have a flying machine at its disposal, so it took a train back to Chicago for its November 13 battle with Northwestern. After IU fell behind 6–0 in the first quarter, Whitaker took it upon himself to lead the Crimson, and he scored a pair of touchdowns and kicked both extra points to lead Indiana to a 14–6 victory. At halftime of the game, Thorpe wowed the crowd with a kicking and punting exhibition, and the fans were crazed just to see the superstar in person.

Following the game, Thorpe's celebrity was too much for a young boy in the crowd to handle. "At Northwestern after the game a little chap came running up to [equipment manager] Uncle Jake Buskirk, who was carrying the ball with which the game had just been won," the 1916 *Arbutus* reported. "The chap touched the ball reverently and then exclaimed exultantly to his fellows, 'Jim Thorpe touched that ball, and so did I!'"

Thorpe's attention, however, wasn't focused on the Crimson by this point. He knew he had to make a living somehow after the IU season ended, and it being football season, Thorpe did the only thing he knew to do. He signed a contract to play for the Canton Bulldogs of the Ohio League after being offered the whopping sum of $250 a game (that's more than $5,800 in 2019 dollars), and Thorpe's first game would be a November 14 battle against the Bulldogs' archrival Massillon Tigers. He took a train from Chicago to Massillon, and he came off the bench to star for the Bulldogs. Canton lost the game 16–0, but more than five thousand fans showed up to watch the game. Most of them had to be there for Thorpe. Although the game was a local rivalry, average attendance for Canton's games prior to the signing had been fifteen hundred fans. After the game, Thorpe headed back to Bloomington.

The final game of the season for the Crimson would be the annual matchup with Purdue, and the town couldn't have been more excited for the game. It was homecoming weekend. With Thorpe on the sideline, it was expected that even more fans and alumni would be making the trip to Bloomington. Adding to the excitement was the thought that Jordan Field would be hosting its last game. Plans had been made to build a new football stadium next to the Men's Gymnasium, which was under construction, and the new field would occupy the space that would eventually become the Bill Garrett Fieldhouse.

Poor weather had chased the Crimson into one of its first indoor practice facilities, a tent set up at the nearby Gentry Farm. The 160-by-300-foot tent was lighted as it would be for a circus performance, and it featured a lined field and goal posts at both ends of the tent. In the week leading up to the Purdue game, Thorpe worked with the kickers for an hour at Jordan Field despite the elements before loading his players into an "auto truck" for the ride to the tent.

The day before the game, Childs made his squad practice on the quagmire that was Jordan Field to get them used to the conditions, and the waterlogged footballs still managed to fly through the uprights on kicks from thirty-five yards out. When the day of the game, November 20, finally arrived, Jordan Field was covered with sawdust to try to absorb the water that had settled on the surface. A bright sun and wind helped a little, but it wasn't enough. Thanks to the construction of two thousand additional seats in the days leading up to the game, a crowd of more than seven thousand packed Jordan Field to see IU battle the Boilermakers.

What they saw was far from the prettiest game in Indiana history, and the rain and snow from the previous three days hampered both teams. Thorpe's kickers weren't very effective considering the fact that drop-kicking the ball was nearly impossible in all the mud, but Purdue managed to boot an extra point en route to a 7–0 win over the Crimson. Thorpe again put on a punting exhibition for the crowd at halftime, but he was careful not to wear himself out. After all, he had a game to play the next day in Canton, Ohio.

Immediately following the game, Thorpe bolted for the train station. He arrived in time for the second battle in three weeks between Canton and

Massillon, and he took over as player-coach of the Bulldogs. He made his presence felt, too, drop-kicking a field goal from forty-five yards out in the first quarter, and he added a place kick of thirty-eight yards in the third quarter to push Canton to a 6–0 victory.

Just like that, the Jim Thorpe Era at IU ended.

Although there were initially some hopes that Childs might bring Thorpe back for the 1916 season, it quickly became clear that Childs had other issues to be concerned about. IU was in the market to make some more changes, and in early December, the Indiana administration hired Ewald O. "Jumbo" Stiehm to take over as director of athletics. Stiehm had made a name for himself as a football coach at Nebraska. With the Crimson making so many upgrades to their athletic programs from a facilities standpoint, it was decided that an experienced leader was needed to take IU into the future. Stiehm was most comfortable on the gridiron, and his arrival spelled the end of Childs's time in Bloomington.

Thorpe and Childs quietly left town, but both would make their marks elsewhere. Childs would never coach football again, but he served in the army during World War I. He was sent to France, and among other jobs, he became the athletic director at the Colombes Stadium in Paris. He left the military with the rank of major, and he became an industrial engineer. He passed away in Washington, DC, in 1960.

Thorpe, meanwhile, would simply go on to be named the greatest athlete of the first half of the twentieth century by the Associated Press. He helped Canton win three Ohio League championships, reportedly sealing the 1919 title with a wind-assisted ninety-five-yard punt late in the game, and he was named president of the American Professional Football Association—a precursor to the NFL—in 1920. Thorpe eventually played for six NFL teams, although he never won a title, and he retired from football in 1928. He also played major league baseball with the Giants, the Cincinnati Reds, and the Boston Braves, compiling a career batting average of .252 in 289 games before retiring from baseball in 1919. He was inducted into the College Football Hall of Fame in 1951 and the Pro Football Hall of Fame in 1963.

Thorpe dabbled in Hollywood, where he made a handful of movie appearances, and he was played by Burt Lancaster in the 1951 film of his life, *Jim Thorpe—All-American*. Thorpe's personal life, meanwhile, was a shambles for most of the rest of his life. He was divorced from Iva in 1925, and he later married twice more. After his playing days ended, Thorpe struggled. He descended into alcoholism, and he worked a number of odd jobs later in life, including serving as a doorman, a ditch digger, and a security guard. When he was hospitalized for lip cancer in 1950, he was broke and had to be admitted as a charity case.

Thorpe recovered from that setback, but he finally succumbed to his third heart attack March 28, 1953, at the age of sixty-four. Following his death, the Pennsylvania towns of Mauch Chunk and East Mauch Chunk purchased his remains from his third wife, buried them, and erected a monument in his honor. The two entities then merged and renamed themselves Jim Thorpe, Pennsylvania, a move that was controversial and the subject of lawsuits from the Thorpe estate until 2015.

In 1982, the IOC reinstated Thorpe's Olympic gold medals from the 1912 games because he was disqualified past the thirty-day time limit for such decisions to be made. Two of Thorpe's children, Gale and Bill, were awarded commemorative medals.

Jim Thorpe's time at Indiana was brief, but his impact on the program during his few months in Bloomington was substantial. He helped create some buzz around the football team, and his presence on the sideline increased attendance—and therefore revenue—at a time when IU was upgrading its facilities. Without Thorpe, IU might not have had the financial confidence to build the IU Fieldhouse (the future Bill Garrett Fieldhouse), and that construction project helped push Indiana to build the original Memorial Stadium. Although some might consider Thorpe to have been more of a sideshow at IU than anything else, the bottom line is that for a few months in the autumn of 1915, the sports world kept an eye on Bloomington, Indiana—a view that it wouldn't normally have had if a god wasn't wandering among the Crimson.

FIGURE 7.1. James Francis "Jim" Thorpe, the most famous athlete in the world, served as an assistant coach for the 1915 IU football team. *IU Archives P0021918*

FIGURE 7.2. Jim Thorpe poses with IU football captain Frank Whitaker (third from left), *Indiana Daily Student* editor Ralph G. Hastings (third from right), and IU football coach Clarence C. Childs (second from right). *IU Archives P0021916*

FIGURE 7.3. Jim Thorpe tutors IU players Harry P. Gray and Clair Hudson Scott in this photo from the 1916 *Arbutus*. IU Archives P0021925

8

Jumbo... and What Might Have Been

During his first five years as the head coach at Ohio State from 2012 to 2016, Urban Meyer's teams were among the most dominant in college football. The Buckeyes went 61–6 overall and 39–2 in the Big Ten, losing no more than two games in any one season with one national championship. Nick Saban, the head coach at Alabama, went 64–7 overall and 35–5 in the Southeastern Conference in that same span, winning a pair of national championships.

During that time, Meyer and Saban were the unquestioned leaders in their profession at the college ranks, and they were paid like it, too. Saban pulled in more than $7 million during the 2016 season, and Meyer made more than $6 million at OSU.

Now, imagine if either Saban or Meyer decided to leave their respective programs to come to Indiana because IU offered them an extra $5,000.

It's a mind-boggling scenario, but once upon a time, that's exactly what happened in Bloomington. One of the best college coaches in the country decided to leave a comfortable, successful situation to take on the challenge of turning IU into winners over the matter of a few hundred dollars. The result? A winning program during one of the most difficult times in IU history.

Ewald O. "Jumbo" Stiehm's decision to come to Indiana in 1916 sent shockwaves through the college football world, and the fascinating and somewhat hard-luck story of the time Indiana poached one of the most innovative college football coaches of his time is one of the great "what-ifs" of IU athletics.

Nebraska football has long been one of the bluebloods of the sport. No, the Cornhuskers aren't what they used to be, but they are still one of just a handful of college programs to win more than eight hundred football games, and the team has gone to a bowl in all but a handful of years since 1962.

That tradition has been decades in the making, obviously, and Nebraska's first real success came from 1900 to 1905 under head coach Walter "Bummy" Booth, who went 46–8–1 during his six seasons in Lincoln. In 1902, his team went undefeated (9–0) and didn't give up a single point. That's not a typo. Nebraska didn't allow a single point to be scored against them during the 1902 season. Following the 1905 season, Booth was making the highest salary of any professor at Nebraska, a fact that rankled some at the school. After earning his law degree, Booth decided to move on, leaving the game entirely.

Nebraska football slid a bit from that high standard under its next two coaches, Amos Foster and W. C. Cole, going 31–12–3 over the next five years. Cole went 7–1 in 1910, but he left over money issues, and he also wasn't interested in becoming a full-time coach—a new rule put in place by the new Missouri Valley Intercollegiate Athletics Association said every member school had to have a full-time head coach. Nebraska needed a full-timer who would come on the cheap, and it found its man in a young coach out of Ripon College who had just put together a 4–3 season in his first year on the job.

Ewald O. "Jumbo" Stiehm was born August 9, 1886, in Johnson Creek, Wisconsin. He grew to a stout six foot four, but it wasn't the size of his body that gave him his unique nickname. It was the size of his feet that reportedly earned him the moniker—one he hated—and he made an even bigger name for himself as a center at the University of Wisconsin, where he was the first Badger to earn first-team All–Big Ten honors. He graduated in 1909, and he spent that fall as a high school coach in Wisconsin. Stiehm moved to Ripon in 1910 to serve as the head coach and director of athletics, a relatively new position at the time. When Nebraska offered him $2,000 to take on the two positions in Lincoln, the twenty-four-year-old jumped at the chance.

For the next six years, Stiehm turned the Cornhuskers into a powerhouse. His first season saw the Cornhuskers go 5–1–2 and tie for first in the Missouri Valley with Nebraska's only loss coming to Minnesota. The next year

Nebraska again tied for first in the league, and the team went 7–1, again losing to Minnesota but winning the final four games of the season.

Stiehm would not lose a game at Nebraska again.

He finally got his revenge on Minnesota in 1913 win a 7–0 win at Nebraska Field thanks to some innovative scouting. During the 1912 game, Stiehm had an assistant coach take photos of the "Minnesota Shift," a precursor to pre-snap motion that baffled the Gophers' opponents, to better prepare his team. The move so angered the Minnesota administration that the two teams wouldn't play again until the 1930s. From 1913 to 1915, the Huskers ran off twenty-seven straight victories, and the one blemish on their record came in a 0–0 tie to South Dakota in 1914.

Stiehm's teams were known as the "Stiehm Rollers," and in 1915, Nebraska went 8–0, won the Missouri Valley title outright for the second straight season, and outscored its opponents 282–39 (nineteen of the thirty-nine points were scored by Notre Dame in a 20–19 NU win). The Huskers were offered an invitation to the Rose Bowl, but the Nebraska Athletic board worried about an overemphasis on athletics and the cost of traveling to Pasadena, California, for the game. The board voted to turn down the invitation to the game, which was already a prestigious event even in those early days.

It was a mistake, one that would cost Nebraska dearly.

Stiehm, who also was the head coach of the Cornhuskers' basketball program, winning three Missouri Valley titles and going 55–14 along the way, was looking for a pay raise, considering the improvements he had made in the athletic programs. Nebraska's 1914–15 athletics revenue totaled around $35,000 in 1915 (nearly $870,000 in 2018 dollars), and Stiehm's leadership and success in football and basketball were big reasons for the windfall. His $3,500 salary was substantial (roughly $86,000 in 2018 dollars), but he was looking for a bit more.

Stiehm wanted Nebraska to commit to the athletics program, which was clearly making the school money and raising the profile of the university in the public eye, by investing in its leader. He asked for $4,250 in annual salary, but the Nebraska Athletic Board balked. The faculty of the university didn't think a football coach should be paid more than full professors (even though Stiehm was, himself, a full professor), and they weren't keen on giving Stiehm more money. Stiehm was operating under a gentlemen's agreement to remain on the job through 1917, but he didn't have a contract.

The athletic board depended on and expected Stiehm to live up to the terms of that agreement. Once again, the athletic board made a miscalculation.

In Bloomington, the first thirty years of the IU football program told a story of mediocrity. Some seasons were good, some were bad (the 1893 and 1894 teams combined to go 1–8–2), and most hovered around .500. James Horne and James Sheldon both had solid runs as head coaches on the gridiron, combining to win sixty-eight games between them from 1898 to 1913.

Following a stellar 1910 season, Sheldon's magic with the Crimson waned. After suffering through back-to-back losing seasons, including just two wins in Big Ten play, Sheldon resigned following the 1913 season (he was awarded a "handsome" watch and chain on the field during the final game of the year in honor of his eight years of service). He was replaced by Clarence Childs, a bronze medalist in the hammer throw at the 1912 Stockholm Olympics, who came to IU after serving as an "all-sports" coach at Wooster College in Ohio.

Childs, unfortunately, didn't fare much better than Sheldon, leading IU to back-to-back 3–4 seasons and going 3–8 in conference play. The Crimson struggled mightily down the stretch of Childs's second season, going 1–3–1 in the last five games of the season, and a 7–0 loss to Purdue in the final game had more than a few asking for a change.

Fortunately, Childs did have some backers on campus. A group with the wonderful name of the "Association of Unorganized Men" adopted a resolution in early December giving Childs a vote of confidence, saying, "We believe that he should not be blamed for faults for which he is not responsible and which have been done contrary to his directions."

Unbeknownst to the public, the wheels were already in motion to make a major change, and Childs's performance on the field had little to do with the moves that were planned.

More than two years earlier, the IU athletics committee had discussed bringing on someone who could serve as the czar of IU athletics. Arthur "Cotton" Berndt, who captained the football, basketball, and baseball teams during his time as a player, served as acting director of athletics and organized intramural athletics from 1913 to 1915, but his power was limited. The plan was on the back burner, but a subcommittee was assigned the task of keeping their eyes open for the right candidate.

In 1915, IU decided to make a significant investment in athletics by constructing a new Men's Gymnasium that would serve as a dedicated athletics facility. The construction would push Indiana athletics to a new level, and the athletics committee decided the time was right to find someone who was experienced and could lead the Crimson into the future.

The athletics committee was determined to recruit the best candidate for the job, no matter the cost. Price was not an object at such an important moment, and 650 miles west in Lincoln, the man IU wanted was ready to listen.

It's not known when IU first made contact with Stiehm about the possibility of leaving Nebraska for Indiana, but IU wasn't alone in its pursuit. At least two other schools were interested in luring Stiehm away, but Stiehm didn't necessarily want to leave. He simply wanted to be fairly compensated for his work.

As Nebraska's athletic board dithered over Stiehm's demands, some Lincoln business owners believed they had come up with a solution. Nebraska could pay Stiehm his usual $3,500, and local businesses would chip in the extra $750 to bring Stiehm to his requested salary of $4,250. The Huskers could hold onto their coach and athletics director without spending another dime, and the local businesses would hold onto a man who had helped the local economy by drawing thousands of football and basketball fans to the area.

It seemed like a perfect solution. The athletic board had other ideas.

Nebraska faculty pressured the board to turn down the proposed arrangement. They were squeamish about entering into such an agreement with outside interests, and besides, it wouldn't ultimately solve the problem of Stiehm being the highest-paid faculty member on campus (even though he already was).

The athletic board turned down the offer from the local businessmen, and Stiehm had had it with Nebraska. The school had blocked his team's opportunity to play in the Rose Bowl, it had turned down his salary request, and it had refused a decent compromise all in the span of a few weeks. Enough was enough.

Indiana, meanwhile, was offering $4,250 in annual salary, the opportunity to be the director of intercollegiate athletics for a growing department, and the university was building a new gymnasium that would be a jewel of the Midwest. On December 5, 1915, Stiehm met with the entire IU athletics committee in Indianapolis to discuss the offer. He liked what he heard and was interested, but there was one catch. Stiehm still had a year left on his gentlemen's agreement, and he would give Nebraska one last shot to hold onto him.

Stiehm went back to Lincoln and asked the athletic board one final time to match the IU offer. The board flatly refused, and Stiehm tendered his resignation effective at the end of the school year.

Stiehm wired Indiana president William Lowe Bryan on December 9 to let him know he had accepted his offer, and an announcement was made late that night that IU had a new athletic director.

"The new director will come to Indiana next year and will assume complete charge of intercollegiate athletics at the University," the *Indiana Daily Student* wrote December 10. "The move does not mean that there will be a sweeping change in the different branches of sports. Indiana's policy will be that which Mr. Stiehm elects. He will have charge of all the coaches, all the administrative direction of affairs in his line."

Stiehm released his own statement in Nebraska to the *Lincoln Star* newspaper, saying, "I would gladly have stayed had the University seen fit to meet the terms offered elsewhere."

Some fans were angry with Stiehm for the betrayal, but he also received plenty of support. Cy Sherman, a writer with the *Lincoln Star*, was firmly in the Stiehm camp and excoriated the Nebraska athletic board for letting Stiehm get away.

"It was inevitable that the pussy-footers and mollycoddles would secretly rejoice over the success of Indiana University in acquiring the services of Jumbo Stiehm," Sherman wrote. "The board realized they have blundered very seriously in letting Stiehm transfer . . . to the Hoosier institution."

IU fans, meanwhile, were thrilled at the hire, believing it proof that Indiana was serious about taking the next step in its athletics.

"I think the selection of Mr. Stiehm as Director of Intercollegiate Athletics in the University is in line with the policy of the University of doing things in a big way," said Adrian Foncannon, the president of the Boosters Club. "Like the erection of a new gymnasium, this action will cause Indiana athletic stock to soar."

Stiehm's departure from Nebraska did not go smoothly. Although he hoped to finish the school year, Nebraska wasn't happy that Stiehm had asked assistant coach R. B. Rutherford to follow him to Bloomington, and that threw a wrench in the works. Nebraska said Stiehm had agreed not to offer Rutherford a job until after the Cornhuskers had made him an offer. Stiehm didn't agree, and he signed Rutherford to an IU contract. Nebraska's chancellor, Samuel Avery, was upset that Stiehm would try to poach another Husker, and the situation looked like it might get ugly.

"Stiehm has notified the chancellor that he is anxious to patch up his differences with the Athletic Board, and the chancellor will in turn call on Stiehm to release Rutherford from his agreement to go to Indiana University with Stiehm as assistant coach," wrote the *Indianapolis Star* on January 7, 1916. "Unless Stiehm grants such a release, the executive committee of the athletic board, it was announced last night, will proceed with its program to dismiss Stiehm as head coach for the balance of the year, which would also mean his dismissal by the university regents as athletic director."

In other words, forget the resignation, Jumbo. You're going to be fired immediately. Stiehm was already pained to be leaving. He didn't want to leave on such bad terms, so the next day he capitulated, releasing Rutherford from his IU agreement. Nebraska countered by offering Rutherford $700 more than IU was offering for his services, and Rutherford accepted the Huskers' offer.

Think about that for a second. Stiehm left Nebraska over the matter of a $750 pay increase, which Nebraska flatly refused to pay. It was willing, however, to offer Rutherford $700 more than Indiana was offering, and it's unlikely Rutherford would have been willing to follow Stiehm for less than he was already making. It appears that Nebraska lost its wildly successful head basketball and football coach / athletic director and kept an assistant coach for basically the same amount of money.

That's not a good trade.

Still, with that situation resolved, Stiehm was cleared to resign, and the board accepted his resignation the following day. Indiana immediately entered into negotiations to try to have Stiehm on campus for spring football practice. The contract he had previously signed with IU was set to take effect August 1, but IU was itching to get him on the gridiron. Oddly, no announcement was ever made regarding Childs's status. It was simply assumed that Stiehm would take over the football coaching duties. Childs, meanwhile, moved over to be the IU track and field coach.

Stiehm ultimately decided to coach spring practice without a contract to get an early start on working with his team. He made his first appearance in Bloomington as a guest of the university and the Boosters Club for the

Indiana state high school basketball tournament, which was being played at the Men's Gymnasium—soon to be renamed Assembly Hall. Stiehm awarded the trophies to the winners of the tournament on March 18, and his presence boosted attendance for the already popular event.

He also looked forward to working with this team.

"If the enthusiasm shown by the men is any criterion, Indiana will certainly have a good team next year," Stiehm told the *Indiana Daily Student*. "The men I have met are all deeply interested—a thing that augers well for the future."

Stiehm also told the Bloomington Chamber of Commerce in a speech that he would "leave nothing undone to beat Purdue," which generated thunderous applause from the group's members.

On April 3, Stiehm welcomed the Crimson to Dunn Meadow and handed out equipment to open spring practice. Thirty-six players showed up, many of whom had never played varsity football before. Such was the power of Stiehm's celebrity, and he expected his players to work from 3:00 to 5:00 p.m. every afternoon until the close of the school year.

The Jumbo Stiehm Era at Indiana had begun.

Remember when we said Stiehm's tenure at IU saw some hard luck? It actually started before the first practice of the fall. Four varsity players, including Archie Erehart, who was described as a "hard-running halfback and a power on defense," were victims of a militia call that sent able-bodied men into the US Army as the United States worked to stay out of World War I. For a team that already had lost eleven lettermen from the year before, losing four more to the military was painful.

By the time fall camp opened September 20, Stiehm had adjusted, and he called on the student body—a robust twenty-six hundred students by this point—to help his players with their training.

"With the assistance of the student body in line with the spirit, interest, and enforcement of training rules, Indiana should have a strong football team this season," Stiehm was quoted as saying in the *Indiana Daily Student*.

In other words, don't offer Stiehm's players booze or keep them up late. They have work to do.

Season tickets for athletics were "selling like cranberries," according to the *Indiana Daily Student*, with more than $750 worth of tickets purchased during the first two days of school. On the field, the military had stolen away a few more players, team captain Freal McIntosh was in the hospital with an attack of typhoid (it was later reported he had suffered a nervous breakdown), and star tackle Lewis Murchie had "scholarship issues" that might leave him ineligible (he did eventually return to the team and earn a letter). Oh, and tackle Russell Hathaway had tonsillitis.

"The coach is making heroic efforts to round out a combination from the material that is left after injuries, graduation, scholarship, and Secretary of War (Newton) Baker have pooled their energies in an attempt to shatter whatever chances the Crimson may have had to possess a veteran football team," the *Indiana Daily Student* said.

On the eve of Stiehm's first-ever game as IU head coach, the *Indiana Daily Student* was adamant in its support.

"The new Crimson Athletic Director accomplished great things at Nebraska," the paper stated. "This year he has taken charge of a team in another school and in different circumstances. He is handicapped by a lack of material, by injuries, and by the ineligibility of several promising candidates. Still this is THE DAY. This is the day that marks the opening of Stiehm's football career at Indiana, and obstacles or not, he is OUT TO WIN."

And win he did. The Crimson hammered DePauw 20–0 on Jordan Field, and optimism was high. Erehart returned from military service to have a good game, and Hathaway bounced back from his illness to star as well. The Crimson wowed fans by throwing the ball, something that hadn't been done much under Coach Childs. Everyone was excited. IU was clearly about to turn a corner.

Or not.

Indiana had the misfortune of playing the University of Chicago, a longtime nemesis, one week after the Maroons were beaten 7–0 by tiny Carleton College of Minnesota. IU was wiped out by the refocused Chicago team 22–0, and the Crimson would manage just thirty-one points and one win during the rest of the season. The one victory came in a 14–3 win over Florida in Bloomington, and IU played to a 0–0 tie with Purdue in West Lafayette. Considering Indiana had dropped five straight to the Boilermakers, a tie wasn't seen as being so bad.

The season ended with IU holding a 2–4–1 record overall with a 0–3–1 mark in Big Nine play. It was far from a successful season, but Stiehm was confident he could make some headway.

Stiehm's 1917 team was all about progress, and the lessons taught during the 1916 season took hold during his second season. Indiana opened with three straight wins for the first time since the 1910 campaign, and IU outscored its opponents 141–0 during those first three outings. It was an offensive explosion like none ever witnessed at IU. Road setbacks at Minnesota and Ohio State took some of the wind out of the Crimson sails, but they closed the season by beating DePauw 35–0 and ripping Purdue in Bloomington 37–0. Indiana finished 5–2, but the Crimson managed to still finish seventh in the Big Nine with a 1–2 conference record.

Still, the progress made was impressive, and it looked like Stiehm's Nebraska history was repeating itself.

The other key development of 1917 had not yet made an impact by the fall of that year, but it certainly would be felt soon. The United States's entry into World War I shredded the football roster of every school in the country, and athletics took a backseat to the war effort. IU still fielded a team in 1918 with Stiehm as a coach, but it wasn't really an Indiana team. It was a service team made up of members of the Student Army Training Corps (a precursor to the Reserve Officer Training Corps, or ROTC), and games were played against opponents such as Kentucky State, Camp Taylor, and Fort Harrison. Stiehm's team went 2–2 that season.

By the way, did we mention that an influenza outbreak that gripped the entire world also made its way to Bloomington, shutting the IU campus from October 10 to November 4? More than three hundred men were hospitalized with the illness on campus, with a hospital being set up at Assembly Hall.

Stiehm was tasked with building his football program once again, and the Crimson went 3–4 in 1919, losing to a Centre College team that featured a star in Alvin "Bo" McMillin, who would go on to become one of IU's most successful football coaches ever. But Stiehm also led the Crimson to a 12–6 win over Syracuse, an Eastern power that was expected to easily dispatch IU when it visited for the final game of the year.

Once again, momentum had been built, but Stiehm couldn't really worry about the future of his football team. Basketball coach Dana Evans had abruptly resigned in August, leaving Stiehm to scramble to find a new leader for IU on the hardwood. He didn't have much luck, so he decided to do the job himself. After all, Stiehm was a successful basketball coach at Nebraska, and there was no reason he couldn't lead the Crimson to victory.

With Everett Dean, IU's first basketball All-American on his side, the duo didn't disappoint.

Indiana and Stiehm posted a 13–8 record overall and went 6–4 in conference play during the 1919–20 season. The thirteen wins tied a school single-season record, and the six conference wins were an IU record at the time. Stiehm hired George Levis prior to the 1920–21 season, ending his one-year reign on the Indiana basketball bench.

IU went 5–2 overall and 3–1 in league play during the 1920 season, and IU beat Purdue 10–7 to close out the year. The Crimson also lost to Notre Dame in Indianapolis in November, falling 13–10. The Irish got back into the game thanks to a touchdown by All-American George Gipp, the last touchdown the "Gipper" would ever score.

The 1921 season started on a high note with a 47–0 win over Franklin and a 29–0 win over Kalamazoo, giving IU seven wins in its previous nine games. Indiana's offense, however, fell apart after those two victories, and the Crimson scored just ten points during the remaining five games of the season. On the bright side, Stiehm did lead Indiana to a 3–0 win over Purdue, giving IU three straight wins over the Boilermakers.

Nobody knew it at the time, but Stiehm had coached his final game.

During the spring and summer of 1922, Stiehm had been bothered by stomach pain. Doctors suspected he was suffering from ulcers—beyond the stress of being IU's athletic director, Stiehm was also overseeing the construction of a house at the corner of Eighth Street and Woodlawn Avenue, just a couple hundred yards away from the Men's Gymnasium and Jordan Field. They advised him to get away from Bloomington at the end of the summer term and enjoy some relaxation before the arduous football season. Stiehm, his wife, Marie, and their two daughters vacationed in Lake Mills, Wisconsin, but his condition didn't improve. Doctors in Lake Mills reportedly ordered him to visit the Mayo Brothers' Clinic in Rochester, Minnesota, where he would be held for observation.

Stiehm wired Indiana requesting a leave of absence in early September, and the news crashed through Bloomington like a thunderbolt.

"Coach Ordered to Hospital," the *Indiana Daily Student* screamed over a picture of Stiehm in its September 6 edition. Despite the concern, observers didn't seem to think the situation was too serious.

"Coach Stiehm has been bothered with stomach trouble for several months, and several physicians have diagnosed the ailment as the result of ulcers," said Dr. W. J. Moenkhaus, a professor of anatomy in the IU School of Medicine. "If this is correct, even in the case of an operation, Coach Stiehm should not be confined to the hospital for more than three weeks. An operation for ulcer of the stomach is no more serious than an appendicitis operation."

It's important to note that Moenkhaus hadn't examined Stiehm and was simply stating his opinion from afar. Still, Stiehm was expected to be back with the team no later than September 20.

But man plans, and God laughs, as the saying goes, and by Monday, September 11, Marie had cabled IU stating that Stiehm had undergone a "serious operation" at Mayo and would be unavailable to coach during the 1922 season. The entire campus quickly rallied to support its coach, and a mass meeting was called both at Assembly Hall (for the men) and at the Student Building (for the coeds) to discuss the situation.

The men held an old-fashioned pep rally, where they resolved to cheer on the football team and use Coach Stiehm as motivation all season. Frank Hanny, the team captain for 1922, was cheered heartily, but nobody drew a louder ovation than IU's first senior manager for football, a journalism student named Ernie Pyle.

More than six hundred women, meanwhile, pledged to attend every practice at Jordan Field the next week, attend every game, and learn the rules of football. They also agreed to a ban on midweek dates, a resolution that had been passed the previous spring.

Just before the start of the meeting, a bulletin reported that Pat Herron, an All-American for Pitt in 1915–16 and an assistant coach to Glen "Pop" Warner at the same school for the previous two seasons, had been hired to coach the team. Negotiations for the job were done long-distance by telephone (a big deal back then), and a telegram sealed the contract. Basketball coach George Levis, who just days before had tendered his resignation after accepting a job to work in the Showers Brothers furniture factory, announced he would stay on as acting athletic director until the situation could be sorted out.

The first practice of the season came September 14, and Herron was welcomed by a throng of fifteen hundred fans in the stands and a whopping seventy-five players in uniform. He quickly got to work and did his best to return Indiana football to normalcy, working his players hard on Jordan Field to prepare for the season opener against DePauw.

Indiana battled DePauw to a 0–0 tie to open the season, and the *Indiana Daily Student* reported that a wheelchair-bound Stiehm had written for information about the football team. The fact Stiehm himself wrote the letter was seen as a positive sign of his recuperation, although there still was no word about when he might be able to return to Bloomington.

The Crimson struggled mightily under Herron, dropping three of four and failing to score a point in any of their losses. The team did get a boost in early November when Stiehm returned home to Bloomington.

"Indiana has displayed a wonderful spirt this year, and I am more than pleased to hear of it," Stiehm said. "I have great respect for Herron and think that he is a mighty good coach."

Stiehm hoped to see IU take on West Virginia that weekend, but if he attended the game, it was not noted in contemporary newspapers.

Stiehm fell out of public view, although he did continue to conduct some administrative work in his role as athletic director. He helped build schedules, he ordered uniforms and equipment, and he generally took it easy, relaxing in his new house. Stiehm also was involved in discussions about the construction of a new football stadium to replace Jordan Field.

One of his duties, however, included the hiring of a new football coach. Herron decided to move on after one season, and in early February, Bill Ingram, a former star for Navy, was hired as IU's permanent head coach. The move was a sign that Stiehm's coaching days were over, although the discreet newspapers of the time didn't comment on what the move meant in terms of his long-term health.

In mid-May, rumors flew that Stiehm would have to take an indefinite leave of absence to travel to either California or Wisconsin to try to regain his once-again failing health. Neither IU officials nor Stiehm himself would comment on the rumors, but the rumor became fact when it was learned that Stiehm had sold his house to a local sorority, Zeta Zeta Zeta.

Late that same month, it was reported that Zora Clevenger, the athletic director at Missouri and a former Crimson star in both football and baseball, had visited Bloomington to be interviewed to replace Stiehm as IU's athletic director. Clevenger wouldn't comment on Stiehm, but it was learned that

Stiehm had asked for a full year's leave of absence, and his position would have to be filled.

A few days later, on June 3, Stiehm officially resigned as director of athletics, citing a "physical inability to perform the duties of the position."

Just like that, the Jumbo Stiehm Era in Bloomington was over.

Two weeks after his resignation, Stiehm returned to his house on Eighth Street and announced to everyone that he was feeling much better. He had once again visited Mayo Clinic, and he was hopeful for his continued recovery. That said, he still wasn't strong.

"Mr. Stiehm will be out in a few days," Marie said. "Although he is feeling better, he is hardly strong enough to see many visitors these hot days."

The truth of the matter is that Stiehm had come home to die.

On August 18, 1923, Stiehm passed away at 8:00 a.m. at his home while surrounded by his family. He was thirty-seven years old. The cause of death was stomach cancer, a terminal diagnosis he had been given eleven months earlier when he made his first trip to Mayo Clinic. Members of his family asked doctors to withhold the information from the public so he might fight the disease in private, but from the moment he learned of his illness, his fate was sealed.

Doctors repeatedly gave Stiehm just weeks to live, but he managed to keep fighting. During the final six weeks of his life, he was unable to eat solid food, and he grew weaker as the days passed. The timing of Stiehm's death also robbed the student body of the ability to honor him en masse. He died while most of the students were away from campus, and the *Indiana Daily Student*, which had passionately supported him since the first rumors of his arrival, wasn't publishing at that time and didn't print a word in memoriam.

With his battle over, Marie and Stiehm's mother and father loaded his body on the Monon Train, and at 12:52 a.m. on August 20, Stiehm left Bloomington for the last time, bound for his burial in Johnson Creek, Wisconsin. Several hundred professors, athletic fraternity brothers, and former players attended services at Allen Funeral Home prior to Stiehm's departure.

Stiehm finished his IU coaching career with a 20–18–1 record. Although nearly a century has passed since his death, Stiehm actually still has a legacy in Bloomington.

His house, which was part of the University Courts historic district, was part of a legal battle to preserve some of the historic homes in Bloomington. It was scheduled for demolition in 2013, but following efforts to save the house, it was moved from the corner of Eighth and Woodlawn to a spot two blocks west on Eighth Street in 2015. It currently serves as a rental property.

Stiehm's legacy at Indiana is one of what-ifs. What if World War I hadn't interrupted his building project? What if the flu didn't impact the university? What if he never became ill? Would IU's football legacy be different today?

It's a question that is impossible to answer. Still, Stiehm's willingness to leave a powerhouse for the challenge of building a program has to be commended, and his legacy, more than one hundred years after his departure from Nebraska, shouldn't be forgotten.

FIGURE 8.1. Ewald O. "Jumbo" Stiehm compiled a 35–2–3 record at Nebraska, including three straight undefeated seasons from 1913 to 1915, before coming to Bloomington to run IU's athletic programs in 1916. *IU Archives P0060573*

FIGURE 8.2. The December 10, 1915, edition of the *Indiana Daily Student* trumpeted the arrival of Jumbo Stiehm's decision to run IU athletics. *IU Archives*

FIGURE 8.3. Jumbo Stiehm's 1916 team went 2–4–1, but he managed to put together a winning record during his six seasons on the sideline.
IU Archives P0025608

FIGURE 8.4. Jumbo Stiehm built a house on what was then the edge of campus along Woodlawn Avenue, but he would only live in it for a short time. *IU Archive P0051877*

FIGURE 8.5. The Stiehm family home still stands in Bloomington, but it was moved two blocks down the street as a historic landmark during the 2000s. *Author photo*

9

What's in a Name?

You may have noticed that this book hasn't referred to the IU athletics teams of the early years as the Hoosiers.

It isn't an accident.

There have been some headlines that used it, but in terms of an official nickname, it doesn't appear. Yet if you travel to literally any IU sporting event, there will be T-shirts and hats and towels and chants all screaming, "Hoosiers!"

The nickname is so ubiquitous that nobody even thinks about it anymore. After all, people from Indiana are known as Hoosiers, and teams from IU are nicknamed Hoosiers. Makes sense, right? It has always been that way, right?

Well, not always, and not for nearly as long as you may think.

This isn't a story about what the word "Hoosiers" means. The term has been around for nearly two hundred years, and the arguments about the origin of the word are long, drawn-out, and don't feature a lot of concrete answers. Suffice to say that somewhere along the way, natives of Indiana picked up the nickname of Hoosiers, and it likely was an insult at first. Slowly, the meaning of the term evolved, Indiana residents started to embrace the word, and the state became known as the Hoosier state.

But that isn't the sole reason IU fans get to chant a catchy nickname these days. After all, there aren't many other states that identify so closely with a singular nickname. New Yorkers are proud to be New Yorkers, but that isn't a distinctive nickname. It's just letting someone know where you live.

That isn't the case in Indiana. Ask someone who grew up in Muncie, Indiana, where they grew up, and they might tell you they're a Hoosier, even if they hate IU with a white-hot passion. Folks from Indiana take great pride in the nickname, but it wasn't always associated with Indiana University athletics.

In fact, it hasn't been associated with IU varsity sports for as long as you might think.

The first thing you need to know about sports nicknames is that, once upon a time, they weren't the rock-solid trademarks we know today. It's pretty rare for sports teams, either collegiate or professional, to make changes. There usually is a franchise move involved (i.e., Montreal Expos becoming the Washington Nationals or the Seattle SuperSonics becoming the Oklahoma City Thunder), or maybe there are philosophical reasons for a name change (the NBA's Washington Bullets changed their name to the Wizards in response to the rampant gun violence in their hometown of Washington, DC). College teams have made adjustments, but outside circumstances, such as complaints about racial overtones, are usually the impetus for those moves.

But that wasn't always the case. During the last quarter of the 1800s into the early quarter of the twentieth century, both college and professional teams routinely made changes to their names, sometimes every couple of years. Take, for example, the long-lost Brooklyn Dodgers. The Dodgers still exist today, of course, as the Los Angeles Dodgers, but in their early years, they were known as the "Trolley Dodgers," thanks to the network of street car lines crisscrossing the streets outside their home ballpark. As time went on, the "trolley" was dropped for the most part, and they became just the Dodgers. But they also were known through the years as the "Grays" (for their uniforms), the "Grooms" (one year a couple of players got married just before the season), the "Bridegrooms" (same reason), the "Superbas" (owner Ned Hanlon was the producer of a Broadway play titled *Superba*) and the "Robins" (for manager Wilbert Robinson). The team always came back to the "Dodgers," until the name finally stuck, mostly because the team started printing the name on its jerseys.

Colleges, meanwhile, often earned their athletic nicknames thanks to newspaper coverage or by the color of their uniforms. Sportswriters of the day often used extravagant, flowery language to describe the games, and they would use whatever descriptive they could to get their point across. For instance, Indiana's cross-country team was known as the "Thin Clads" at times well into the twentieth century, not as a consistent, official nickname, but because writers wanted to use a word other than "runner" (cross-country runners didn't—and still don't—wear much, so they are thinly clad).

And, let's face it, during the early years of intercollegiate athletics, writers didn't quite know how to go about covering the sports they watched. It wasn't their fault. Organized athletics wasn't really a part of the American landscape in any widespread form until the late 1800s. Baseball teams thrived, but football was a relatively new sport, and basketball was in its infancy. Difficulty in traveling made intercollegiate athletics especially rare, although they started to become more common late in the nineteenth century.

In the 1880s, Indiana University's colors were established as cream and crimson, and they remain so to this day. As such, the team's uniforms and sweaters were usually crimson, or they were crimson and cream striped. Sportswriters of the time, being the original bunch they were, called the team the "Cream and Crimson," or, more frequently, the "Crimson."

The first known reference to IU's sports teams as the "Hoosiers" came in the October 27, 1899, edition of Tennessee's *Nashville Banner*. Under the headline "Vanderbilt Meets Indiana Eleven," a subhead read, "Hoosiers One of the Strongest Western Teams." But that use of "Hoosiers," much like other uses of the term that occasionally would pop up in newspapers covering Indiana athletics, served more as a general term for the players than an actual team nickname.

For example, prior to IU's 1910 game with Chicago, one that saw Indiana score its first-ever win over its conference rival, the *Daily Student* wrote the following line:

"Kelley, who has been assisting in the line coaching at Marshall Field, brought news of Hoosier cleverness and speed, despite the fact Sheldon's men used only a few rudimentary plays against DePauw."

The same coverage of the game went on to say:

"The Indiana slogan for several years has been: 'Beat Chicago this time or never.' The saying is getting to be a football chestnut, in a way, but just the same there is a magnificent chance for the Crimson this year."

The actual coverage of the game from the *Daily Student* identified the team as the "Cream and Crimson" and "the Crimson." No mention of "the Hoosiers" is anywhere to be found. So it would remain for years, even as the 1917 *Arbutus* called IU the "Hoosier University."

"While the people of other states are loyal, the Hoosier loves his soil with a passion that ever remains wherever future residence may take him," the *Arbutus* stated. "Anyone who answers to the same proud name is his neighbor and welcome to his goods. And Indiana University is the Hoosier University."

IU may have been the "Hoosier University," but its teams weren't.

In the early 1920s, however, that started to change.

Indiana's first effort to find a new nickname was something of a disaster. A 1921 game against Harvard saw both teams nicknamed the "Crimson," and when IU returned from its 19–0 drubbing, a movement was started to make a change to try to set Indiana athletics apart. Unfortunately, the suggestions didn't exactly blow anyone away.

The Glory of Old IU, a book on the history of IU athletics by Bob Hammel and Kit Klingelhoffer, reports that the nicknames suggested included the "Arbutarians," the "Bloodhounds," the "Red Clovers," the "Fighting Foxes," the "Unlicked Cubs," and, strangest of all, the "Wampus Cats." The last suggestion seems to be a nod toward the teams from the Cambridge City, Indiana, high school, which was known by the same name.

Indiana wisely passed on all the suggestions and stuck with the "Crimson" for the time being. But the hiring of a former IU star would help send Indiana athletics on the path to a legendary name.

Zora Clevenger was a Hoosier through and through. He was born in Muncie, Indiana, December 12, 1881, and he arrived in Bloomington in 1900 to go to school at IU and play a little football. He was a three-sport star from 1900 to 1903, lettering in football, basketball, and baseball, captaining all three squads as a senior.

After graduating, he served as IU's head basketball and baseball coach from 1904 to 1906, and he filled in, for all practical purposes, as the director of athletics during the 1905–6 school year. He went on to serve as football, basketball, and baseball coach at Nebraska Wesleyan, Tennessee, and Kansas State from 1907 to 1921, and he served as athletic director at Kansas State and Missouri along the way. When IU athletic director Ewald "Jumbo" Stiehm passed away in 1923, following an illness, Indiana turned to Clevenger to take over its athletic department.

The draw of returning to IU was too strong for Clevenger to pass up, and he arrived in the summer of that year. One of his first orders of business was to hire a new football coach to help boost the status of the struggling program. He turned to former Navy star William "Navy Bill" Ingram, who had posted a 6–3 record at William & Mary in 1922.

With his new coach in tow, Clevenger went on the road during the summer to promote IU athletics and Indiana football in an effort to drum up support for the Crimson. Fan enthusiasm wasn't exactly high, and with a new stadium being built—it would become the original Memorial Stadium—Clevenger wanted to do a little fundraising while elevating the awareness of the athletic department.

During the events around the state, a lot of speeches were made, and somewhere along the way, either Clevenger or Ingram—it isn't clear which one—said his team would be filled with "scrappin' Hoosiers," that is, players who came from the state of Indiana. By the time football practice began, the phrase started to catch on.

The October 4, 1923, edition of the *Indiana Daily Student* announced a meeting to be held in Assembly Hall the next day, a men's-only event that would serve as a de facto pep rally for the football team.

"Men to Fan Smoldering Embers of Hoosier Fight," the *Indiana Daily Student* headline read. The subhead ran, "Big Crimson Mass Session, to Boost Support of Scrappin' Indiana Eleven, Set for Tomorrow Night at Assembly Hall."

The next day, the *Indiana Daily Student* gave an update on the event, writing, "There, every thought will be turned toward tomorrow's initial test of the ex-Navy star's team of Scrappin' Hoosiers."

In Saturday's edition, a story in the *Indiana Daily Student*, previewing the game between the Crimson and DePauw to open the season, read, "Although outweighed man for man, Captain Stew Butler will lead 2,000 pounds of Crimson brains and muscle in their grim and determined effort to prove themselves worthy of the title, 'Scrappin' Hoosiers.'"

Later in the same article, the *Indiana Daily Student* wrote, "The Scrappin' Hoosiers, although handicapped by injuries, will not be without dangerous backs and powerful linemen."

A nickname was slowly being nurtured. Unfortunately for "Navy Bill" and the Crimson, the enthusiasm didn't help on the field. IU lost its season opener to the Tigers 3–0, giving DePauw—a team also known as the "Methodists"—its first win over Indiana in nearly thirty years.

Still, the narrow loss by an injury-plagued Crimson squad did nothing to kill the notion that Ingram's team was a group of fighters. That said, Indiana was far from favored for the next weekend's game, a battle against Northwestern University in Indianapolis (IU's records say the game was played in Evanston, but it wasn't; it was played in Washington Park in Indy, the current site of the Indianapolis Zoo.).

It would prove to be a critical day in Hoosier history.

In what was billed as the first "real test" for Ingram's "Scrappin' Hoosiers," IU managed to pull off a win thanks to an eighty-yard touchdown run by Lawrence Marks in the first five minutes of action, and Indiana's defense battled to keep Northwestern at arm's length. The Crimson gave up 276 yards of total offense, and the Purple managed to cross the goal line on a run, but NU missed the extra point, and IU made the edge stand up for a 7–6 win.

The *Indiana Daily Student* used the term "Scrappin' Hoosiers" in its coverage, but more importantly, Chicago papers were on hand to cover NU. Always looking for a good angle, the Chicago sportswriters latched on to the nickname, and suddenly a loving, local term was blasted across the country along with the news of IU's shocking win.

From that point on, the name stuck. Newspapers still called IU's sports teams the "Crimson," but the "Scrappin' Hoosiers" and just the "Hoosiers" started to be sprinkled into the mix. Meanwhile, back in Bloomington, the nickname continued to pick up steam.

The 1924 *Arbutus* grabbed onto the moniker with gusto. One page runs the phrase "Scrappin' Hoosiers" alongside some photos from the season, and the football report praises Ingram's squad as well: "Indiana's huge Memorial Stadium rising slowly tier upon tier; a new Indiana spirit fanned into flames by a rejuvenated student body—these were the transformations of 1923 that formed a setting for the battles of a grim and fighting Crimson eleven," the *Arbutus* wrote. "On the hard turf of Jordan Field they won a new name that sums up briefly a short season's history—'The Scrappin' Hoosiers.'"

The *Arbutus* later reported on the Northwestern game: "Washington Park was the scene of the famous Northwestern battle. There gridiron fans sat through sixty minutes of thrilling play while a grim fighting machine, outweighed man for man, stood off dangerous Purple onslaughts and emerged with a 7–6 win. There the Crimson warriors first received their title, 'The Scrappin' Hoosiers.'"

Of course, the papers say IU had been given the nickname prior to the actual game, but again, it only caught on in the public consciousness after the Northwestern win.

Not that the "Scrappin' Hoosiers" managed to capitalize on the good feelings following the NU victory. The next week against Wisconsin, Ingram's squad was hammered 52–0 by Wisconsin, and the team managed just a 3–4 record on the season.

But the genie was out of the bottle, and IU fans rallied around a name that was theirs and theirs alone. No longer would Indiana have to share a nickname with any other school. By the next season, the nicknames "Crimson" and "Scrappin' Hoosiers" were being used interchangeably to describe the football team. As time passed and football players continued to play other sports, the nickname slowly came to describe all the athletic programs at Indiana.

The "Hoosier" nickname hasn't been tinkered with much over the years, save for the dropping of "Scrappin'" and the addition of "Hurryin'" during the Branch McCracken days. Multiple attempts have been made to supplement the nickname with a physical mascot ranging from a bison to humans wearing costumes, but those have never stuck.

To this day, the Hoosier name is somewhat of a mystery. But for a century, IU's athletic teams have gone by the same nickname, and it has provided a solid link from the present to the past for Indiana fans around the globe. No one might be certain about what a Hoosier is or where the nickname came from, but it's clear that Indiana fans are happy with the tradition of the nickname and won't be looking to make any additions or subtractions anytime soon.

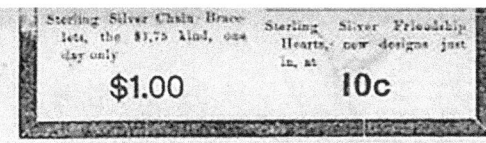

FIGURE 9.1. The October 27, 1899, *Nashville Banner* headline marks the first known use of the nickname "Hoosiers" for an IU athletic team, but the name wouldn't be commonly used until the 1920s.

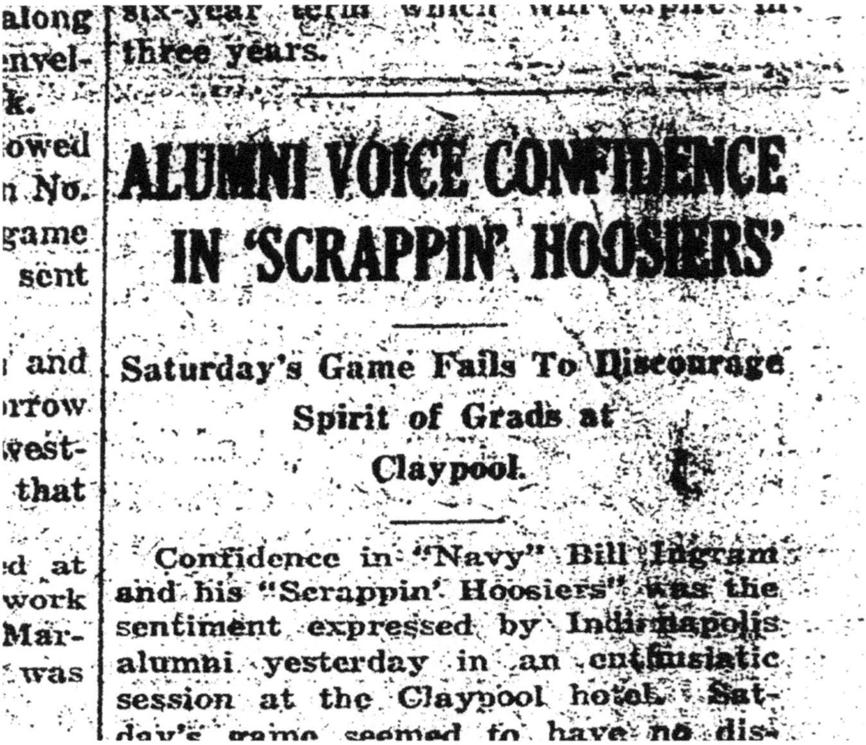

three years.

ALUMNI VOICE CONFIDENCE IN 'SCRAPPIN' HOOSIERS'

Saturday's Game Fails To Discourage Spirit of Grads at Claypool.

Confidence in "Navy" Bill Ingram and his "Scrappin' Hoosiers" was the sentiment expressed by Indianapolis alumni yesterday in an enthusiatic session at the Claypool hotel. Sat-

FIGURE 9.2. By this October 9, 1923, issue of the *Indiana Daily Student,* the Hoosier nickname was starting to catch on. *IU Archives*

10

The Old Stolen Bucket

It happens every time Indiana wins back the Old Oaken Bucket.

The Hoosiers roar across the field in search of their prize, a reward for all its hard work and determination, tangible proof that IU will own bragging rights on one of the oldest rivalry trophies in college sports for the next twelve months.

When Purdue wins the Bucket back, the process is reversed. And whichever team owns the trophy for a given year, it makes sure the trophy leaves the stadium with them.

After all, that hasn't always happened.

The Old Oaken Bucket made its first appearance in 1925 during IU's first season in the original Memorial Stadium. The Chicago chapters of the Purdue and Indiana alumni organizations got together to discuss a suitable trophy for the rivalry game, and it was resolved that an old oaken bucket would be found to serve the purpose.

Legend has it the trophy was found on the Bruner family farm between Kent and Hanover in southern Indiana. The bucket may have been used in a well, but the family history claimed it was used by General John Hunt Morgan and his "Raiders" during the Civil War. There's no way to prove that, but it makes for a good story. The two alumni organizations decided the winner of each game would get either a bronze *I* or *P* attached to the bucket in remembrance of that year's winner. As luck would have it, the first link on the Old Oaken Bucket is a combined "I-P" link to commemorate the 0–0 tie, topping off a gorgeous trophy with an appropriate link.

That first tie game was followed by four straight Purdue wins. In fact, the series wasn't even close. The Boilermakers outscored IU 91–20 in the first four Bucket games, and in the 1930 season, Purdue looked like it was in good shape to hold onto the Bucket for a fifth year. The Boilers headed into the 1930 game with a 6–1 record and had won fourteen of their last fifteen games dating back to the previous season.

Indiana, meanwhile, was, well, Indiana. The Hoosiers struggled mightily on the gridiron in 1930 and had won just one game, a season-opening 14–0 win over Miami (Ohio). Since that victory, IU had scored exactly one touchdown all season, and that came in a 7–7 tie with Oklahoma A&M (later to become Oklahoma State). Indiana hadn't managed to score a point since that October 11 battle and had been outscored 115–21 on the season. With a road trip to Purdue looming to mercifully close the season, IU looked like it was in trouble.

Purdue was all but assured a victory, but Indiana had other plans.

Then, as now, records for both teams could be thrown out when the two ball clubs battled. It didn't matter to IU fans that the Hoosiers were so bad. A win over Purdue would make the season worthwhile, and students gathered Thursday, November 21, in Bloomington for a pep rally that would set the campus on fire—quite literally. A torchlight procession brought students and fans to the annual burial of Ole Jawn Purdue in front of the Men's Gymnasium for a yell session and a bonfire.

"The greatest pep session ever held on the Indiana campus took place last night amid bursting bombs and glaring lights to convince [head coach] Pat Page and his Scrappin' Hoosiers that the Indiana student body is back of them to the last man," the *Indiana Daily Student* wrote the next day. "It was not the winning of a conference championship, nor the conquering of a great foe that was necessary to goad the student body to action. They assembled because they knew that Page and his men needed their help."

Fireworks were sent into the night air. Chants of "Beat Purdue" were heard. The band played. It was, according to the *Indiana Daily Student*, the largest gathering of students for a pep rally in years.

It may have been the largest gathering in years, but it didn't necessarily draw attention from the bulk of the students. The *Bloomington Telephone*'s report on the pep rally was impressed by a crowd of roughly five hundred people, but it wondered where the other three thousand students who were on campus were that evening.

"Spirit, it seems, has been so long dormant on the IU campus that an attempt to revive it for even so important a battle as the clash with Purdue meets with only mediocre success," the *Telephone* wrote.

On the morning of game day, some five hundred fans, students, and alumni loaded onto a special train at the Bloomington Monon Railroad station for the trip to West Lafayette at 8:00 a.m., six hours prior to kickoff. The train was festooned with decorations, and a steamboat whistle was installed to loudly announce IU's presence when the train passed through towns and arrived at Purdue. "Scrappin' Hoosiers" was written in crimson on the side of the coal car, and it was outlined in cream-colored paint. The Old Oaken Bucket was painted on the side of the engine cab, and the interlocking IU logo was on the front.

It was quite the sight.

The train rolled into West Lafayette on time, and more than fifteen hundred Hoosier fans packed IU's section at Ross-Ade Stadium to cheer on their heroes.

For once, they had something to cheer about. Purdue got on the board early, scoring a touchdown in the first three minutes of the game, and the Hoosiers looked like they were en route to another beating. The Boilermakers missed the extra point, however, and Indiana managed to turn up the defense. Both teams were held scoreless until early in the fourth quarter. At the Purdue thirty-five-yard line, Indiana threw a short pass to Vic Dauer, and he weaved through the Purdue defense to score IU's first touchdown in six weeks. The score tied the game and sent the IU faithful into a frenzy. On the sideline, senior kicker Ed Hughes pulled off his sweatshirt and trotted onto the field to attempt the extra point. The ball was snapped, and Dauer—IU's holder—had to stretch to nab the pigskin, but he got it down just in time for Hughes's toe to rip through the ball and send it end over end through the middle of the goalposts. IU led 7–6, but it had to hold on for another ten minutes.

Purdue's passing attack was feared, but the Hoosiers held, and they had a shot at icing the game with just minutes left after driving to the Purdue fifteen-yard line. A run up the middle gained five yards, but on second down, a short pass was intercepted at the Boilermakers' five-yard line, giving Purdue life.

The Boilermakers, however, didn't have a comeback in them. IU continued to shut down the passing game, and the clock expired without a Purdue score, giving the Hoosiers their first Old Oaken Bucket win.

Too bad the actual trophy wasn't on hand.

Purdue couldn't imagine actually losing to Indiana, and it hadn't bothered to bring the Old Oaken Bucket to Ross-Ade Stadium. It did already have a bronze "P" ready to put on the Bucket, and both the letter and the trophy were at the Purdue Union awaiting that night's celebratory mixer dance.

Indiana decided to turn its attention elsewhere. The freshman football team, some team reserves, and some fans headed across the field and tried to ring Purdue's "Victory Bell," which was being protected by the Boilermakers' Gimlet Booster Club.

Naturally, that didn't go over well with the Purdue faithful, and a brawl broke out. Punches flew, some noses were broken, and blood was spilled, but the bell went untouched.

Coach Page and his Scrappin' Hoosiers were scheduled to be on the 7:00 p.m. train back to Bloomington, where the celebration was already raging—bonfires had been started in the town square, and President William Lowe Bryan dispatched guards to Assembly Hall to ensure no one would set it on fire—and the team didn't have time to head over to the mixer dance to pick up the Bucket. That job would fall to an IU student by the name of Charley Hoover, who was in West Lafayette as a representative of the Indiana Student Union. The head of the Purdue Student Union, Lloyd Vallely, stood on the stage at the mixer dance, tasked with giving the Old Oaken Bucket to Indiana for the first time ever. The Purdue students at the dance were silent as Vallely handed the trophy to Hoover, and they glared at Hoover as he held the Bucket up and thanked the Purdue students.

Already feeling nervous over the notion of being one of the only IU people at the dance and the person who would take off with the trophy, Hoover looked at the Purdue students and decided he didn't want to walk out of the hall with the trophy in his hands. Hoover worried for his safety. He handed it back to Vallely and said it might be best for the Bucket to change hands another day. Hoover returned to Bloomington without the Bucket, and the following Monday, he called Valley to arrange for the transfer of the trophy. A celebratory dance was scheduled at IU for Monday night, and Hoover knew he needed to get the Bucket to Bloomington.

Valley was understanding, and he promised to send it by express train to Indianapolis, where it could be picked up by Hoover or some other IU representative. Hoover agreed and hung up, thinking everything would be all right.

The weather that Monday was ugly, as it often is in Bloomington in late November. It was cold, windy, and rainy, and Hoover wasn't excited about driving to and from Indianapolis in the nasty conditions.

Maybe, just maybe, Hoover could draft someone who was already planning to come to Bloomington that night to pick up the Old Oaken Bucket.

Enter John Bookwalter, an owner of the Bookwalter-Ball-Greathouse printing company of Indianapolis. Hoover called Bookwalter and told him of his predicament, and Bookwalter gave him the bad news that he wasn't coming to Bloomington that night. The good news was that Bookwalter was willing to go to the express station and pick up the Old Oaken Bucket and then put it on a bus bound for Bloomington. The bus would arrive in town at 9:00 p.m., just in time for the dance to begin.

All of this seems a little spineless and lazy on Hoover's part, but the bottom line is he had a plan to get the Bucket to Bloomington. Everything was arranged, and Hoover relaxed.

When the dance began, a band called Bud Dent and his Collegians played a song called "The Old Oaken Bucket" at full volume. The bus arrived in Bloomington on schedule but with one hiccup.

The Old Oaken Bucket wasn't on the bus. In fact, nobody knew where the Bucket was or who had it. It was missing.

Early the next morning, Hoover called Bookwalter to find out where it was. Bookwalter was a little confused. After all, he had already given it to IU's representatives. See, Bookwalter went down to the express station and picked up the Bucket from the train. There he was met by . . . well, we'll let the *Indiana Daily Student* explain.

"A delegation of Indiana students with IU stickers and pennants adorning their suitcases, coats and laundry bags had met him at the station and told him that they had been sent from Bloomington to get the Bucket," the *Indiana Daily Student* wrote. "Naturally, Mr. Bookwalter, having been convinced by the victory-flushed faces and shining Cream and Crimson stickers that this certainly was a representative group from the IU campus, surrendered the prized trophy." The group, dressed up as IU representatives, took the Old Oaken Bucket and walked off into the night, never to be seen or heard from again.

The situation had advanced beyond Hoover's head—in all honesty, it seems like he was in over his head to begin with—and Bookwalter called James Fesler, president of the IU board of trustees. Bookwalter explained the situation, and Fesler quickly decided to call in the big guns.

His first move was to involve Harry G. Leslie, a former Purdue player who just so happened to be the governor of Indiana at the time. The athletics directors from both schools—Nelson Kellogg for Purdue and Zora Clevenger for Indiana—were contacted, and a conference was set up in Lafayette with Leslie, Kellogg, Clevenger, Fesler, Bookwalter, and poor Charley Hoover to discuss what would come next. Meanwhile, some other key information emerged.

It seems that Purdue's sacred "Victory Bell" had been stolen in the early morning hours of Sunday, November 24, just after the end of the mixer dance. The bell had been mounted on a cart, and it seems someone had hitched the cart to their car and headed south.

Naturally, Purdue students immediately suspected Indiana students, and no fewer than five freight cars were chartered for the next train headed toward Bloomington. The idea was that Purdue fans could fill the train cars and go get the bell back.

That posse never had a chance to explode in violence. Sometime Monday morning, the bell was found in a roadside ditch near Wingate, Indiana, about twenty-five miles south of West Lafayette. The cart, it seems, had crashed and headed off the road, leaving the bell a bit beat up. Still, it was found. One item, however, was missing. The clapper, that piece of metal that hangs inside the bell, was nowhere to be found.

The mystery stretched on for days and became national news. Amateur sleuths suggested all kinds of theories, but it was clear that this was a case of theft. Setting up a time for the governor and all the other luminaries to gather for a conference took time, and by early December, the Bucket was still missing, the passage of time only adding to the story. The involvement of the governor showed that the theft of the Bucket wasn't being taken as a happy college prank. This was a serious matter, and there was going to be a legal price to pay when the mystery was solved.

Then, in the early morning hours of December 4, an elderly man quietly walked to the loading platform of the *Lafayette Journal and Courier* and deposited a crate on the dock. Employees of the newspaper saw him from a distance, but they made no effort to stop him. When they went to the dock to inspect the crate, they found the Old Oaken Bucket inside, completely undamaged. Nothing was missing, the links were still in the chain, and the trophy was none the worse for wear.

There also was no note, no explanation for where the Bucket had been. There was nothing—just an old man, a crate, and a mystery.

Indiana didn't care. The Bucket had been found, and headlines screamed the news.

"OLD OAKEN BUCKET IS DISCOVERED," blared the *Indiana Daily Student*. The Bucket had been recovered, but it would still take a few days for it to get to Bloomington. Clevenger was headed to a meeting with the Big Ten in Chicago over the weekend, and he told Purdue he would personally pick up the trophy on his way back to Bloomington to ensure nothing else happened to it. Finally, on Monday, December 8, the Old Oaken Bucket, which Indiana had won from Purdue sixteen days earlier, arrived on the IU campus. Precautions were taken to make sure nobody would steal the bucket anytime soon.

"The real Indiana-Purdue trophy, representative of supremacy on the gridiron, will be placed on display in a special-constructed glass 'cage' in the catalog room of the University library," the *Indiana Daily Student* reported. "It is temporarily on display in the library. When queried as to what would be done with the bucket the remainder of the year, Mr. Clevenger stated that it probably would be placed in some strong vault but that it may be taken out for any occasions that call for its display."

Nobody tried to steal the Old Oaken Bucket over the next year, but the Boilermakers earned it back in 1931, scoring a 19–0 win in Bloomington. Purdue would go on to win the Bucket in five of the next eight meetings, but Indiana dominated the 1940s by winning seven of ten games. The Boilers would dominate the series from 1948 to 1975, with IU winning just three games and tying once, but the series has remained relatively competitive ever since.

The Bucket, by the way, was stolen on at least three other occasions, including in 1958 and the late 1960s and early 1970s, and it has been the target of failed attempts at other times. But in this day and age, stealing the Old Oaken Bucket has fallen out of favor. The trophy has remained safe for decades, and the only way for someone to own it is to earn a victory on the field.

Two questions still remain: Why was the Old Oaken Bucket stolen? And who stole it?

Let's answer the second question first. Nobody knows who actually stole the Old Oaken Bucket, and that secret likely lies in the grave of the person or people involved in the theft. As for the elderly man who is said to have returned it, he could have been someone involved in the theft or, more likely, the father of someone involved in the situation who wanted to return the Bucket before anybody could get into real trouble over it. After all, the theft rose to the level of the governor, and someone was going to be arrested if the culprits were found.

Exactly who stole the Bucket, and the identity of those people dressed in IU shirts and stickers and pennants, remains a mystery that might stay that way forever.

As to why the Bucket was stolen, it has been suggested that the trophy was kidnapped in response to the theft of the Victory Bell and, maybe more importantly, the clapper in the bell. The theory goes that the Bucket was going to be held hostage until the clapper was returned.

That theory sounds plausible, and it's plausible that once the heat was turned up by the coverage of the theft, and it became clear that hiding a bell clapper is a heck of a lot easier than hiding the distinctive Old Oaken Bucket, robbers could get cold feet. After all, what were they going to do with the Bucket? Put it on their mantle? Not a good idea if you're trying not to get caught for a theft that has caught the governor's attention.

Ultimately, it doesn't matter who stole the Bucket or why they did it. The Old Oaken Bucket was returned intact, and the theft only added to the lore surrounding one of college football's most famous trophies.

FIGURE 10.1. A special car taking fans from Bloomington to West Lafayette for the 1930 Old Oaken Bucket game was a gaudy cream-and-crimson celebration. *IU Archives P0030456*

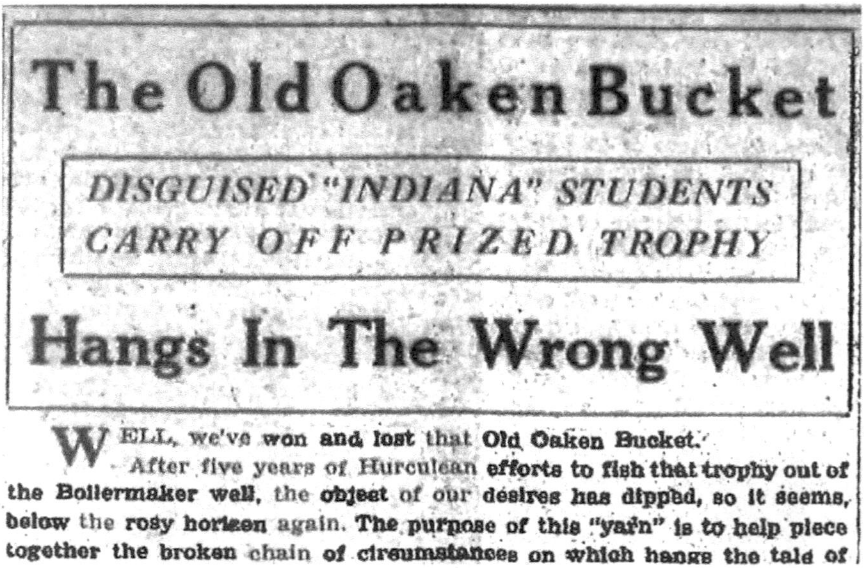

The Old Oaken Bucket

DISGUISED "INDIANA" STUDENTS CARRY OFF PRIZED TROPHY

Hangs In The Wrong Well

WELL, we've won and lost that Old Oaken Bucket. After five years of Hurculean efforts to fish that trophy out of the Boilermaker well, the object of our desires has dipped, so it seems, below the rosy horizon again. The purpose of this "yarn" is to help piece together the broken chain of circumstances on which hangs the tale of

FIGURE 10.2 The theft of the Old Oaken Bucket sent shock waves across the state and had the November 25, 1930, *Indiana Daily Student* buzzing.

Sources

CHAPTER 1

Annual Reports of Indiana University for 1867–69; 70–75.
Bloomington Telephone, 1891–92.
Clark, Thomas D. *Indiana University, Midwestern Pioneer, Volume I—The Early Years*. Bloomington & London: Indiana University Press, 1970.
"I" Men's Notes, Vols. I–III, 1916–19.
Indiana Daily Student, 1867–96.
Indiana University Alumni Quarterly Volume 1, p. 415.
Indiana University Board of Trustees Minutes, 1883–92.
The Indiana Alumnus, 1926.

CHAPTER 2

Bloomington Courier, 1900–1901.
Bloomington Telephone, 1897.
Bloomington World, 1900.
Clark, Thomas D. *Indiana University, Midwestern Pioneer, Volume II—In Mid-Passage*. Bloomington & London: Indiana University Press, 1973.
Hammel, B., & Klingelhoffer, K. *Indiana University: Glory of Old IU*. Champaign, IL: Sports Publishing Inc., 1999.
Indiana *Arbutus*, 1902.
Indiana *Arbutus*, 1923.

Indiana Daily Student, 1897–1916.
Nathan, Angel. "Beyond the First: Early African-American Athletic Experiences at IU." Accessed June 29, 2018. http://blogs.iu.edu/bicentennialblogs/2017/08/16/beyond-the-first-early-african-american-athletic-experiences-at-iu/comment-page-1/.
PFRA Research. "No Christian End!: The Beginnings of Football in America." The Journey to Camp: The Origins of American Football to 1889. Accessed June 29, 2018. http://www.profootballresearchers.org/articles/No_Christian_End.pdf.

CHAPTER 3

Bloomington Telephone, 1896–1938.
Bloomington World, 1896.
Indiana *Arbutus*, 1901.
Indiana *Arbutus*, 1911.
Indiana *Arbutus*, 1919.
Indiana Daily Student, 1896–1903.
Indiana University Biennial Report, 1892.
Indiana Alumni Magazine, April 1958.
IU *Alumni Quarterly*, January 1915.
IU *Alumni Quarterly*, April 1915.
IU *Alumni Quarterly*, Winter 1938.
Springfield College. "Where Basketball Was Invented: The History of Basketball." Accessed June 29, 2018. https://springfield.edu/where-basketball-was-invented-the-birthplace-of-basketball.

CHAPTER 4

Miller, John J. *The Big Scrum: How Teddy Roosevelt Saved Football*. New York: Harper Perennial, 2011.
Indiana Daily Student, 1909–10.

CHAPTER 5

Bloomington Telephone, April 18–25, 1913.
Bloomington World, April 25–26, 1913.
Hammel, B., and K. Klingelhoffer. *Indiana University: Glory of Old IU*. Champaign, IL: Sports Publishing Inc., 1999.
Indiana Daily Student, April 23–26, 1913.
Indiana University Football Record Book, 2017.
Indiana University Basketball Record Book, 2017.

CHAPTER 6

Clark, Thomas D. *Indiana University, Midwestern Pioneer, Volume II—In Mid-Passage*. Bloomington & London: Indiana University Press, 1973.
Hammel, B., and K. Klingelhoffer. *Indiana University: Glory of Old IU*. Champaign, IL: Sports Publishing Inc., 1999.
Indiana *Arbutus*, 1920.
Indiana Daily Student, 1903–28.
Rochester Sentinel, April 1, 1903.
Slutzky, Jason. "The Purdue Train Wreck of 1903: A Football Rivalry Touched by Tragedy." Indiana University Bloomington. Accessed June 29, 2018. https://blogs.libraries.indiana.edu/iubarchives/2013/11/25/purdue-train-wreck1903/.

CHAPTER 7

Hammel, B., and K. Klingelhoffer. *Indiana University: Glory of Old IU*. Champaign, IL: Sports Publishing Inc., 1999.
Indiana *Arbutus*, 1916.
Indiana Daily Student, 1915.
The Indianapolis Star, 1915.
Kellams, Dina. "Jim Thorpe: World's Greatest Athlete." Indiana University Bloomington. Accessed June 29, 2018. https://blogs.libraries.indiana.edu/iubarchives/2011/04/11/jim-thorpe-worlds-greatest-athlete/.
"Students and Thief's Wife; Yale Football Tackle Takes Up Collection for Her in Court." *New York Times*, October 28, 1910.
Buford, Kate. *Native American Son: The Life and Sporting Legend of Jim Thorpe*. Lincoln: University of Nebraska Press, 2012.

CHAPTER 8

Bloomington World, August 19–20, 1923.
Indiana Daily Student, 1916–23.
Sehert, Walt. "The Nebraska Steihmrollers." *McCook (NE) Gazette*, December 28, 2009.
Nebraska Cornhuskers Football Record Book, 2016.
"Ex-Indiana Mentor Expires." *Indianapolis Star*, August 19, 1923.

CHAPTER 9

Hammel, B., and K. Klingelhoffer. *Indiana University: Glory of Old IU*. Champaign, IL: Sports Publishing, 1999.

Indiana Arbutus, 1917.

Indiana Arbutus, 1924.

Indiana Daily Student, 1910–23.

"Vanderbilt Meets Indiana Eleven." *Nashville (TN) Banner*, October 27, 1899.

CHAPTER 10

Cook, Brad. "Sincerely Yours: The Origins of the Old Oaken Bucket." Indiana University Bloomington. Accessed June 29, 2018. https://blogs.libraries.indiana.edu/iubarchives/2016/11/15/sybucket/.

Indiana Daily Student, November–December 1930.

"Old Oaken Bucket." Purdue University Traditions. Accessed June 29, 2018. https://purdueuniversitytraditions2.weebly.com/old-oaken-bucket.html.

Index

Page numbers in italics indicate illustrations.

Assembly Hall; *See* Men's Gymnasium (1896)
Athletic Association, 34, 53, 107–110, 124
Auto polo, 40–41

Ballantine, William Gay, 13
Berndt, Arthur "Cotton," x, 74, 87–89, 91, *94–95*, 98–99, 117, 151; basketball coach 92; team captain 78, 81, 83
Bookwalter, John, 181–182
Bryan, William Lowe, 5, 8, 36, 38, 101, 108–110, 113–116, 153, 180; groundbreaking 119, 121, *129*; inauguration 55, 66

Camp, Walter, 25
Carpenter's Shop; see Men's Gymnasium (1892)
Central Committee, 112–113

Clevenger, Zora, 33, 34, 109, 160, 171–172, 182–183
Cravens, John W., 36, 115–116, 119
Crean, Tom, 97
Crimson nickname, 31–34, 39–41, 58, 65, 74–75, 77–78, 80–93, 98–99, 110, 116, 125–126, 132, 135–144, 151–152, 155–158, 160, 170–174; school colors 12

Dean, Everett, 126, 158
Dunn Cemetery, 28, 31
Dunn Farm, 28
Dunn, Moses, 11, 27

Eagleson, Preston, 27, 44–45

Fesler, James, 114, 182
Foundation Day, 2, 15, 66, 124–125
Founders Day, 2

191

Gill, Andrew "Andy," 74, 77, 80–84, 86–93
Gonterman, Madison G., 27, 29

Herron, Pat, 159–160
Hoosiers, xii, 168, 170–173, 175, 177–180
Hoover, Charley, 180–182
Horne, James H., 107–109, 151; basketball coach, 60–62, 70; football coach, 32–34; life, 29
Horner, Jack, 112–113

Indiana College; see Indiana University naming of
Indiana Memorial Union, ix, 17, 41
Indiana University, xi–xii, 12–13, 18, 29, 52, 54–55, 57, 65, 80, 111, 113, 136, 153–154, 169–171; baseball, 6, 8–10; founding of, 1, 4; Jordan Field, 37–38; Men's Gymnasium (1917), 116–119; naming of, 1–3
Indiana University: Midwest Pioneer, 26
Ingram, William "Navy Bill," 160, 172–174
Insight Bowl, 97
Intercollegiate Football Association, 25
IU Athletic Park, 10, 27–28

Jones, Aquilla, 4–5, 8–9
Jordan Field, ix–x, 30–42, 46–49, 74, 76–80, 82, 84–89, 91, 105, 107, 110, 115–116, 121, 127, 132, 135–137, 139, 142, 156, 158–160, 173; baseball diamond, 31, 39–40; conditions, 34, 36; construction, 28; activities, 40–41; end of, 1959, 42; ice skating, 35–37
Jordan River, 28, 30–31, 38–39; Spanker's Branch, 28–29

Kemmer, A.E., 121–122, 124–125

Leslie, Harry, 107, 182
Levis, George, 158, 159
Lockridge, Bruce, 109
Lynch, Bill, 97

Maxwell, James D., 12–14
Maxwell, Leslie "Doc," 65–67, 72
McCracken, Branch, 174
McDonald, Malcom Andrew "Mack," 4–9, *19*
McMillin, Alvin "Bo," 157
Men's Gymnasium (1892), 16, 23, 50
Men's Gymnasium (1896), 16, 28, 53, 55–57, 66, 78, 98, 110, 117, 155; Assembly Hall, x–xi, 58–61, *68–69*, 78, 98, 117, 155, 157, 159, 172, 180; construction, 51–52
Men's Gymnasium (1917), 28, 37, 40, 58, 119, 121, *130*, 139, 142, 151, 158, 178; activities, 123–128; groundbreaking 115–117
Memorial Stadium (1925), ix–x, 40, 105, 125, 144, 172–173, 177
Memorial Stadium (1960), xi, 106, 112
Morgan, General John Hunt, 177

Naismith, James, 14, 60
New College Building, 11

Old Oaken Bucket, 58, 177–86

Powell, Arthur, 98
Purdue train crash (1903), 106–107
Pyle, Ernie, ix, 41, 159

Records, Thomas, 60–64
Rutherford, R. B., 153–154

Schultz, Carl, 99–100
Scrappin' Hoosiers, 172–174, 178–180
Seminary Square, x, 2, 5, 9–11, 21–22, 27, 29
Shea, Joseph Hooker, 113–114, 121
Sheldon, James, x, 35–36, 74–75, 77–80, 82, 84–92, 109, 131, 151
Simon Skjodt Assembly Hall (1971), 50, 97, 106, 112, 127
Spanker's Branch; *see* Jordan River
Stiehm, Ewald O. "Jumbo," 143, 148–162, *163–167*, 171
Strange, Ernest, 62, 64
Swain, Joseph, 28, 30, 51, 53–55

Thorpe, James Francis "Jim," x, 132–144, *145–147*
Trimble, George Frank "Duke," 75–77, *94*

University Baseball Club, 5

William Leon (Bill) Garrett Fieldhouse, 40, 123, 142, 144
Wilson, Thomas, 10
Woodford, Arthur B., 11, 25–26, 43
Wylie, Andrew, 3, 5
Wylie, Theophilius, 5, 11
Wylie House, 3

Ken Bikoff is a 1997 graduate of Indiana University's School of Journalism and has spent more than twenty years as a professional writer covering the NFL, the NBA, and college basketball. He has spent the past fifteen years focusing on IU football and basketball. He is currently the cohost of the postgame call-in show for Hoosier football on the IU Radio Network, and he is the host of the *Peegs Podcast* on Peegs.com. He is also a communication specialist for the IU Luddy School of Informatics, Computing, and Engineering. Ken and his wife, Lauren, have two young boys, Nick and Charlie.

www.ingramcontent.com/pod-product-compliance
Lightning Source LLC
Chambersburg PA
CBHW032043150426
43194CB00006B/403